NEWCASTLE/BLOODAXE POETRY SERIES: 17

# THE MIGHTY STREAM

# NEWCASTLE/BLOODAXE POETRY SERIES

1: Linda Anderson & Jo Shapcott (eds.)
*Elizabeth Bishop: Poet of the Periphery*

2: David Constantine: *A Living Language*
NEWCASTLE / BLOODAXE POETRY LECTURES

3: Julia Darling & Cynthia Fuller (eds.)
*The Poetry Cure*

4: Jo Shapcott: *The Transformers*
NEWCASTLE / BLOODAXE POETRY LECTURES
[Delayed title]

5: Carol Rumens: *Self into Song*
NEWCASTLE / BLOODAXE POETRY LECTURES

6: Desmond Graham: *Making Poems and Their Meanings*
NEWCASTLE / BLOODAXE POETRY LECTURES

7: Jane Hirshfield: *Hiddenness, Uncertainty, Surprise*
NEWCASTLE / BLOODAXE POETRY LECTURES

8: Ruth Padel: *Silent Letters of the Alphabet*
NEWCASTLE / BLOODAXE POETRY LECTURES

9: George Szirtes: *Fortinbras at the Fishhouses*
NEWCASTLE / BLOODAXE POETRY LECTURES

10: Fiona Sampson: *Music Lessons*
NEWCASTLE / BLOODAXE POETRY LECTURES

11: Jackie Kay, James Procter & Gemma Robinson (eds.)
*Out of Bounds: British Black & Asian Poets*

12: Sean O'Brien: *Journeys to the Interior*
NEWCASTLE / BLOODAXE POETRY LECTURES

13: Paul Batchelor (ed.)
*Reading Barry MacSweeney*

14: John Halliday (ed.)
*Don't Bring Me No Rocking Chair: poems on ageing*

15: Gwyneth Lewis: *Quantum Poetics*
NEWCASTLE / BLOODAXE POETRY LECTURES

16: Anne Stevenson: *About Poems and how poems are not about*
NEWCASTLE / BLOODAXE POETRY LECTURES

17: Carolyn Forché & Jackie Kay (eds.)
*The Mighty Stream: poems in celebration of Martin Luther King*

NEWCASTLE/BLOODAXE POETRY SERIES: 17

# THE
# MIGHTY STREAM

## POEMS IN CELEBRATION OF
## MARTIN LUTHER KING

EDITED BY
CAROLYN FORCHÉ & JACKIE KAY

BLOODAXE BOOKS

ISBN:   978 1 78037 392 8

First published 2017 by
Newcastle Centre for the Literary Arts,
Newcastle University,
Newcastle upon Tyne NE1 7RU,
*in association with*
Bloodaxe Books Ltd,
Eastburn,
South Park,
Hexham,
Northumberland NE46 1BS.

**www.bloodaxebooks.com**
For further information about Bloodaxe titles
please visit our website or write to
the above address for a catalogue.

Supported using public funding by
**ARTS COUNCIL
ENGLAND**

Cover design: Neil Astley & Pamela Robertson-Pearce.

Printed in Great Britain by Bell & Bain Limited, Glasgow, Scotland, on
acid-free paper sourced from mills with FSC chain of custody certification.

# CONTENTS

# PREFACE

It is now fifty years since Martin Luther King received an Honorary Doctorate of Civil Law from Newcastle University, on that occasion giving his last speech outside the United States before his assassination. Newcastle was the only university in the United Kingdom to have so honored Dr King, whose remarks were not planned, but given extemporaneously and without notes on the subject of his chief concerns at the time: poverty, racism, and war. Implicit in all of these is the question of justice. In his appeal that day, Dr King proclaimed that '...the world will never rise to its full moral or political or even social maturity until racism is totally eradicated... it may be true that morality cannot be legislated but behaviour can be regulated. It may be true that the law cannot change the heart but it can restrain the heartless. It may be true that the law cannot make a man love me but it can restrain him from lynching me; and I think that is pretty important also. And so, while the law may not change the hearts of men, it does change the habits of men if it is vigorously enforced, and through changes in habits, pretty soon attitudinal changes will take place and even the heart may be changed.'

He called for alliance with those attempting 'to deal forthrightly and in depth with these great and grave problems'. The film of this speech was recently discovered in the archives of the University, and is itself a poem crying out against the complicity of silence, because, as Dr King has warned, 'there comes a time when silence is betrayal'. This lost speech has inspired our commemorative collection of poetry gathered from both sides of the Atlantic. On the North American shores, we celebrate this anniversary in a perilous time, but as Dr King has insisted: 'The ultimate measure of a man is not where he stands in moments of comfort and convenience but where he stands at times of challenge and controversy.'

'I have a silence to be rightened,' writes Tyehimba Jess in a poem that joins this symphony of utterance, these voices of dissidents, exiles, refugees, veterans of wars and warriors against racial and social injustice, on behalf of the poor, and for peace. They appear here, arranged by decade of birth, though not strictly chronologically. Our call went out for poems that might address the crises named by Dr King that November day in Newcastle fifty years ago: poverty, racism, and war. In the words spoken by poet Elizabeth Alexander on the occasion of President Barack Obama's inauguration, may these works together constitute a 'Praise song for struggle, praise song for the day.../praise song for walking forward in that light.' And as Dr King urged at Newcastle, may they help bring about a time 'when all over the world justice will roll down like waters and righteousness like a mighty stream'.

CAROLYN FORCHÉ

# PREFACE

Living through these strange and surreal times makes me think about values. When I was growing up, it seemed that racism might be something we could fight and that we would win. I never imagined, none of us naively did, that we would now be living through times when Martin Luther King's famous speeches and interventions feel prescient. We don't just look back at the impact the Civil Rights movement had on us all. We look forward with it. His words echo and ring through our own time, those of us who still dare to dream. Martin Luther King is a man who speaks for all time. Newcastle University gave him his only honorary degree in this country. Watching the footage of him receiving it, and his beautiful and eloquent speech that day is electrifying.

I was brought up in a house of certain values. I went on anti-apartheid marches, on CND marches. I wrote Christmas cards to Nelson Mandela and the other prisoners in South Africa. I had a FREE ANGELA DAVIS poster on my bedroom wall, I grew up knowing of Martin Luther King's famous 'I had a dream' speech and of the world grief when he was assassinated. I turned to the poetry of African Americans in my teens. I couldn't find then any black British writers – so I read Nikki Giovanni and Audre Lorde, Langston Hughes and Sonia Sanchez, Alice Walker and Sapphire. I identified with them. They helped me grow up and form my own identity. It took a little longer before I came across, in my early twenties, the poetry of Afro-Caribbean writers from or based here – poets like Jean 'Binta' Breeze, Fred D'Aguiar, James Berry, John Agard, Grace Nichols. Poetry finds a way of making connections across the waters and the seas. Poets dare to dream. I'm delighted that this anthology has brought together these poets from America and Britain in honour of Martin Luther King. He still walks with us. He still crosses over the bridge. We're still sitting down at the table with him. These poems show just how much we care about our world and our future.

JACKIE KAY

# ACKNOWLEDGEMENTS

We wish to thank members of the Newcastle Centre for the Literary Arts: Linda Anderson who had the original idea for this anthology and oversaw its coming together; John Challis who meticulously and with huge dedication worked on all aspects of the process, and Theresa Muñoz whose last minute help was invaluable. We also wish to thank Neil Astley of Bloodaxe Books for his vision and exemplary editorial skills.

This anthology has been produced for Freedom City 2017 (www.freedomcity.com), a city-wide celebration across Newcastle marking fifty years since Dr Martin Luther King, Jr was awarded an honorary degree at Newcastle University on 13 November 1967.

You can watch the film of Dr King's Newcastle speech here: http://www.ncl.ac.uk/congregations/honorary/martinlutherking/

A full transcript can be found here: http://bit.ly/2wbkUn6

I

# NIKKI GIOVANNI

## In the Spirit of Martin

This is a sacred poem...blood has been shed to consecrate it...wash your hands
...remove your shoes...bow your head... *I... I... I Have A Dream*

That was a magical time...Hi Ho Silver Away... Oh Cisco/Oh Pancho... *Here
I Come To Save The Day...* I want the World to see what they did to my boy...
No... No... No I'm not going to move... *If we are Wrong... then the Consti-
tution of the United States is Wrong...* Montgomery... Birmingham... Selma...
Four         Little         Girls... Constant Threats... Constant Harassment...
Constant Fear... SCLC... Ralph and Martin... Father Knows Best... Leave It
To Beaver... ED SULLIVAN... *How Long... Not Long*

But what... Mr Thoreau said to Mr Emerson... are you doing out?

This is a *Letter from Birmingham City Jail...* This is a eulogy for Albany... This
is a water hose for Anniston... This is a Thank you to Diane Nash... This is a
flag for James Farmer... This is a HowCanImakeItWithoutYou to Ella Baker...
This is for the red clay of Georgia that yielded black men of courage... black
men of vision... black men of hopes... bent over cotton... or sweet potatoes...
or pool tables and baseball diamonds... playing for a chance to live free and
breathe easy and have enough money to take care of the folks they love... *This
is Why We Can't Wait*

That swirling Mississippi wind... the Alabama pine... that Tennessee dust
defiling the clothes the women washed... those hot winds... the lemonade
couldn't cool... that let the women know... we too must overcome... this is for
Fannie Lou Hammer... Jo Ann Robinson... Septima Clark... Daisy Bates... All
the women who said Baby Baby Baby I know you didn't mean to lose your
job... I know you didn't mean to gamble the rent money... I know you didn't
mean to hit me... I know the Lord is going to make a way... *I know I'm Leaning
On The Everlasting Arms*

How much pressure... does the Earth exert on carbon... to make a diamond...
How long does the soil push against the flesh... molding... molding... molding
the moan that becomes a cry that bursts forth crystalline... unbreakable... price-
less... incomparable... Martin... *I Made My Vow To The Lord That I Never*

14

*Would Turn Back*... How much pressure do the sins of the world press against the heart of a man who becomes the voice of his people... He should have had a tattoo, you know... **Freedom Now**... or something like that... should have braided his hair...carried his pool cue in a mahogany case...wafted that wonderful laugh over a plate of skillet fried chicken...drop biscuits... dandelion greens on the side

This is a sacred poem... open your arms... turn your palms up... feel the Spirit of Greatness... and be redeemed

# TOI DERRICOTTE

## On the Turning Up of Unidentified Black Female Corpses

Mowing his three acres with a tractor,
a man notices something ahead – a mannequin –
he thinks someone threw it from a car. Closer
he sees it is the body of a black woman.

The medics come and turn her with pitchforks.
Her gaze shoots past him to nothing. Nothing
is explained. How many black women
have been turned up to stare at us blankly,

in weedy fields, off highways,
pushed out in plastic bags,
shot, knifed, unclothed partially, raped,
their wounds sealed with a powdery crust.

Last week on TV, a gruesome face, eyes bloated shut.
No one will say, 'She looks like she's sleeping,' ropes
of blue-black slashes at the mouth. Does anybody
know this woman? Will anyone come forth? Silence

like a backwave rushes into that field
where, just the week before, four other black girls
had been found. The gritty image hangs in the air
just a few seconds, but it strikes me,

a black woman, there is a question being asked
about my life. How can I
protect myself? Even if I lock my doors,
walk only in the light, someone wants me dead.

Am I wrong to think
if five white women had been stripped,
broken, the sirens would wail until
someone was named?

Is is any wonder I walk over these bodies
pretending they are not mine, that I do not know
the killer, that I am just like any woman –
if not wanted, at least tolerated.

Part of me wants to disappear, to pull
the earth on top of me. Then there is this part
that digs me up with this pen
and turns my sad black face to the light.

# YUSEF KOMUNYAKAA

## Our Side of the Creek

We piled planks, sheets of tin,
& sandbags across the creek
till the bright water rose
& splayed both sides,

swelling into our hoorah.
Our hard work brought July
thrashers & fat June bugs
in decades of dead leaves.

Water moccasins hid in holes
at the brim of the clay bank
as the creek eased up pelvic
bones, hips, navel, & chest,

to eyelevel. When the boys
dove into our swim hole
we pumped our balled fists
to fire up their rebel yells.

The Jim Crow birds sang
of persimmon & mayhaw
after a 12-gauge shotgun
sounded in the deep woods.

If we ruled the day an hour
the boys would call girl cousins
& sisters, & they came running
half-naked into a white splash,

but we could outrun the sunset
through sage & rabbit tobacco,
born to hide each other's alibis
beneath the drowned sky.

# Ota Benga at Edankraal

Maybe it was hog-killing time
    when he arrived in Lynchburg,
        Virginia, several lifetimes behind him,

the old smell of the monkey house
    at the New York Zoological Gardens
        receding, a broken memory left.

Not sure of the paths & turns
    taken, woozy in a swarm of hues,
        he stood in Anne Spencer's garden

surrounding the clapboard house,
    but when she spoke he came back
        to himself. The poet had juba

in her voice, & never called him
    Artiba, Bengal, Autobank, or
        Otto Bingo. Her beds of tiger

lilies, sweet peas, & snapdragons
    disarmed him. Her fine drawl
        summoned rivers, trees, & boats,

in a distant land, & he could hear
    a drum underneath these voices
        near the forest. He never spoke

of the St Louis World's Fair
    or the Bronx Zoo. The boys
        crowded around him for stories

about the Congo, & he told them
    about hunting 'big, big' elephants,
        & then showed them the secret

of stealing honey from the bees
    with bare hands, how to spear fish
        & snare the brown mourning dove.

One night he sat in the hayloft,
    singing, 'I believe I'll go home.
        Lordy, won't you help me?'

A hoot owl called to the moon
    hemmed in a blackberry thicket,
        & he bowed to the shine of the gun.


## The Soul's Soundtrack


When they call him Old School
he clears his throat, squares
his shoulders, & looks straight
into their lit eyes, saying,
'I was born by the damn river
& I've been running ever since.'
An echo of Sam Cooke hangs
in bruised air, & for a minute

the silence of fate reigns over
day & night, a tilt of the earth
body & soul caught in a sway
going back to reed & goatskin,
back to trade winds locked
inside an 'Amazing Grace'
which will never again sound
the same after Charleston,

South Carolina, & yes, words
follow the river through pine
& oak, muscadine & redbud,
& the extinct Lord God bird
found in an inventory of green
shadows longing for the scent
of woe & beatitude, taking root
in the mossy air of some bayou.

Now Old School can't stop
going from a sad yes to gold,

into a season's bloomy creed,
& soon he only hears Martha
& the Vandellas, their dancing
in the streets, through a before
& after. Mississippi John Hurt,
Ma Rainey, Sleepy John Estes,

Son House, Skip James, Joe
Turner, & Sweet Emma,
& he goes till what he feels
wears out his work boots
along the sidewalks, his life
a fist of coins in a coat pocket
to give to the recent homeless
up & down these city blocks.

He knows 'We Shall Overcome'
& anthems of the flower children
which came after Sister Rosetta,
Big Mama Thornton, & Bo Diddley.
Now the years add up to a sharp
pain in his left side on Broadway,
but the Five Blind Boys of Alabama
call down an evening mist to sooth.

He believes to harmonise is
to reach, to ascend, to query
ego & hold a note till there's
only a quiver of blue feathers
at dawn, & a voice goes out
to return as a litany of mock
orange & sweat, as we are sewn
into what we came crying out of,

& when Old School declares,
'You can't doo-wop a cappella
& let your tongue touch an evil
while fingering a slothful doubt
beside The Church of Coltrane,'
he has traversed the lion's den
as Eric Dolphy plays a fluted
solo of birds in the pepper trees.

# ROBERT PINSKY

## Poem of Disconnnected Parts

At Robben Island the political prisoners studied.
They coined the motto *Each one Teach one*.

In Argentina the torturers demanded the prisoners
Address them always as *'Profesor'*.

Many of my friends are moved by guilt, but I
Am a creature of shame, I am ashamed to say.

Culture the lock, culture the key. Imagination
That calls boiled sheep heads 'Smileys.'

The first year at Guantánamo, Abdul Rahim Dost
Incised his Pashto poems into styrofoam cups.

*'The Sangomo says in our Zulu culture we do not*
*Worship our ancestors: we consult them.'*

Becky is abandoned in 1902 and Rose dies giving
Birth in 1924 and Sylvia falls in 1951.

Still falling still dying still abandoned in 2005
Still nothing finished among the descendants.

I support the War, says the comic, it's just the Troops
I'm against: can't stand those Young People.

Proud of the fallen, proud of her son the bomber.
Ashamed of the government. Skeptical.

After the Klansman was found Not Guilty one juror
Said she just couldn't vote to convict a pastor.

Who do you write for? I write for dead people:
For Emily Dickinson, for my grandfather.

*'The Ancestors say the problem with your Knees*
*Began in your Feet. It could move up your Back.'*

But later the Americans gave Dost not only paper
And pen but books. Hemingway, Dickens.

Old Aegyptius said Whoever has called this Assembly,
For whatever reason – that is a good in itself.

O thirsty shades who regard the offering, O stained earth.
*There are many fake Sangomos. This one is real.*

Coloured prisoners got different meals and could wear
Long pants and underwear, Blacks got only shorts.

No he says he cannot regret the three years in prison:
Otherwise he would not have written those poems.

I have a small-town mind. Like the Greeks and Trojans.
Shame. Pride. Importance of looking bad or good.

Did he see anything like the prisoner on a leash? Yes,
In Afghanistan. In Guantánamo he was isolated.

Our enemies 'disassemble' says the President.
Not that anyone at all couldn't mis-speak.

The *profesores* created nicknames for torture devices:
The Airplane. The Frog. Burping the Baby.

Not that those who behead the helpless in the name
Of God or tradition don't also write poetry.

Guilts, metaphors, traditions. Hunger strikes.
Culture the penalty. Culture the escape.

What could your children boast about you? What
Will your father say, down among the shades?

The Sangomo told Marvin, *'You are crushed by some*
*Weight. Only your own Ancestors can help you.'*

23

## Mixed Chorus

My real name is Israel Beilin. My father
Was a Roman slave who gained his freedom.
I was first named Ralph Waldo Ellison but

I changed it to the name of one of your cities
Because I was born a Jew in Byelorussia.

I sit with Shakespeare and he winces not.

My other name is Flaccus. I wrote an essay
On the theme You Choose Your Ancestors.
It won't be any feeble, conventional wings

I'll rise on – not I, born of poor parents. Look:
My ankles are changed already, new white feathers

Are sprouting on my shoulders: these are my wings.

Across the color line I summon Aurelius
And Aristotle: threading through Philistine
And Amalekite they come, all graciously

And without condescension. I took the name
Irving or Caesar or Creole Jack. Some day they'll

Study me in Hungary, Newark and L.A., so

Spare me your needless tribute. Spare me the red
Hideousness of Georgia. I wrote your White
Christmas for you. And my third name, Burghardt,

Is Dutch: for all you know I am related to
Spinoza, Walcott, Pissarro – and in fact my

Grandfather Burghardt's first name was Othello.

## MARILYN NELSON

## Boys in the Park

*Chicago, 1967*


In town to do good works, filled with our own
virtue, five of us joined a game of catch
with boys who looked like the boys who'd teased
us at recess, who called girls dumb, yanked pigtails,
burped, and were generally as annoying as younger
brothers. But, barely chest-high, these were a swarm
of fingerling piranhas, of little photo
rapists in t-shirts and sneakers, racing around us
with knowing hands, then running off
down the parkslope, tossing the ball,
laughing, children of our people, leaving us
to our shame.

Yes, they had poverty, futility,
unequal opportunity, childhood
neglect and abuse; they had hopelessness,
the past and future an unrelieved sentence
of humiliation and meaninglessness;
they had understandable grievances
against a society which treats some
with unjust contempt. (In yesterday's news
a samaritan walked six blocks to buy
gas for three people stranded in their car.
They threw it on him and tossed a lit match.
He was black, they were white, one was pregnant.)
And we had been sheltered by white-collar
fathers who insisted on A's, mothers
who read Langston Hughes aloud at bedtime.
Innocent as midwest hicktown white girls,
we had love, homes, hope. We had all the luck.
But is virtue the flip side of blessing?
Is malevolence excused by despair?

Engulfed in a storm-cloud of boys, I looked down
on twenty close-shorn heads. In an instant I remembered
Dr King's voice from the pulpit:
*Freedom*, hands rose under my skirt;
*equality*, my breasts were pinched.
The day before, I'd knelt on a sidewalk
singing, and a woman pushing a stroller
had called me a cocksucking nigger whore.
*Justice* I willed myself *peace* to unknow
*conscience* the evil I saw *dignity*
pinpricked in her *faith* blue *humanity* eyes.
They were boys, just boys, nine or ten years old.

# KEVIN BOWEN

## Dioxin Song

Somewhere in the sky their healthy bodies float above us.
Somewhere they swim in an air better than any we will ever know.
The chemical scent gone, the burning.

Children sent back to live this time in their true bodies,
their pure, unsullied bodies, nothing in their cells
but the clear waters they see falling at the edge of the skies.

How many of them?  How many each day
slipping out from flesh: children born into those twisted forms,
children with fins where arms ought to be, toes and legs

sprouting like flowers from their chests?
In a film, I watched two boys with giant heads,
heavy ovoid eyes, snouts for noses, sit gently

before a thatched house in a village. Eighteen and twenty
years old, still poised like children, they edged in close
beside their father who spoke with absolute calm

about the ways he cared for them. Moments later, a young woman
with clear, dark eyes leaned forward, tried to smile
but couldn't. All through the interview she struggled

patiently to get her two daughters,  born without eyes, –
to sit up straight on the mat beside her. What many
forms love takes. A friend told me once

the story of the birth of his first child: how he climbed the wall
of the hospital so he could look in on his wife,
He was so filled with joy, he said, to see it healthy,

he was half-way home before he realised he hadn't
checked to see if the child was a boy or a girl.
He asked if I had ever seen the fetuses

kept in jars in the hospital in the south,
those babies with the wizened faces
staring out through the yellow glaze of formaldehyde.

The image of their gorgon heads, their humped
and fish-like torsos woke him
up at night, he said.

Somewhere they too float in the sky above us.
Somewhere what doesn't die
lives on in silent rage.


## 'About as close as you can get...'


In the photo they carry him across the yard strapped to a stretcher.

'A prisoner being returned from interrogation,'
the caption reads.

'All appropriate means are used in interrogations'
the Secretary of State and Secretary of Defense assure.

Routine techniques may include:

'covering the suspects' heads with black hoods for hours at a time',
'forcing prisoners to stand or kneel in uncomfortable positions
in extreme cold or heat'.

Senior officials insist interrogation rely solely
on what they consider
'acceptable techniques'.

Some of these may consist of:

'deprivation of sleep and light deprivation',
'the temporary withholding of food, water,
access to sunlight and medical attention'.

Women are sometimes used 'in order to humiliate men'.
Interrogations are often conducted 'outside the jurisdiction of American Law'.

'Pain alone will often make people numb and unresponsive,'
says the deputy director of the Center for the Study of Terrorism
and Political Violence at St Andrews.

In this case, painkillers were withheld.
He had been shot several times.

He demanded eight hours sleep, which were granted,
but not consecutively.

'Not quite torture, but about as close as you can get,'
an official is quoted as saying.

FANNY HOWE

## Heart Copy

In Anatolia (where I've never been) the saffron hills seem to border
an ocean and the orange car lights mime the same in the sky.

A hospital and autopsy room and the body are being ripped apart without respect:

A heart slapped in a bucket: dirt in the trachea and lungs.
A hospital worker better than a physician to the body.
Good with her hands in a bucket
like a worker at the till in a supermarket.

She said we have everything in reverse.

As an example a red corpuscle flew from the corpse
onto the collar of the detective
who could  name the properties in a drop of blood
and this way prove there is no God.

## The Feast

Roast lamb. Mint jelly.

Sprigs scenting the meat like incense.

A burnt offering is the only one
the Lord accepts.

Not rare or well done.

But burned, burned, burned.

The plurality of the apple
makes us dare to pulp.

Can we breed lambs
without seeing meat?

This is my body
I cannot eat.

Once the lambs
were tender towards the shepherd.

Now they shall want
to take his eyes off them.


Lamb unremembered so many
hanging, and days spent fenced in.

Split lips for laughter to be released or songs
or bleats, memories ejected onto canvas or score
or brains where they burned
their impressions in.

Spray, dispersion, atoms, up close for crying.
They had no bleat without a mother to create and hear it.


The others are strong.
Not the lamb –

its fleece, eyes, meat, tongue, heart
are made for a factory.

At first there were folds.
Now there are millions of mass-produced

packages of flesh.

Bundles of wool
hang on hooks like the rags
of laborers that hung on pegs.

# MARILYN HACKER

## Calligraphies III

Fifty years later
the Ravensbrück survivor
got out her notebooks.

The Gestapo seized her trunks
of thesis chapters with her.

They were lost. She lived –
not a Jew, a resistant.
Ninety, she rewrote

dialogues from the Aurès
under the tents or the stars.


\*

Under freezing rain
we walked back from the film, up
the rue de Charonne.

The doctor turned journalist
was an old comrade of hers,

got out of prison
a year before she did, but
he served sixteen years.

What choice? And now? We argued
to the women's shelter door.


\*

Shelter of a book
and the lamp's upholstered swath
across the pillow.

Midnight-lit in a window,
a young man washes dishes

in his underwear.
His girlfriend watches the news.
The summer moon's full

of memory and presage
above the same old rooftops.


\*

Same old swollen gums
in Beirut, New York, Paris.
Antibiotics

and a dentist appointment
providential in August.

Sick and tired of sick
and tired. Which minor ailment
is a harbinger?

What about the clear azure
and the solar palm of noon?


\*

If the cupped palm
held a capsule to suppress
remorse and regret

for words not written or said,
for inert acedia,

would you swallow it
and forget what you might have
done if you were not

nibbling the short hours away,
mired in the mire of your days?

*

Days of translation –
how many words will you keep
and use them again?

Your friend doesn't want to speak
her mother tongue any more.

Not loss of love but
necessity, a new life
in a new language

and nine square meters, not walls
of books, bright kitchen, garden.


*

Told in a kitchen
as she diced a red onion;
read in a kitchen

while rice swelled on the fire;
argued out in a kitchen

over coffee cups
from different hemispheres –
remembered kitchens,

their yellow or brick-brown walls,
their transnational garlic.


*

A bulb of garlic,
six rust-gold shallots, and ten
russet potatoes.

Coins, words, above my cloth bag.
'Your words heal my heart,' said the

bearded greengrocer,
maybe twenty. 'Egyptian,
by his accent,' my

brother from Isdoud told me
as we walked home from market


*

The common market
turns into Fortress Europe.
Tiny Kurdish boy

washed up on a Turkish beach
whose family name was changed

'Shenu' to 'Kurdi'
like the 'Israels', 'Sarahs'
who, with their lost names,

were, if lucky, refugees
seventy years earlier.

# MIMI KHALVATI

## Afterwardness

An eleven year old boy from Aleppo
whose eyes hold only things no longer there
– a citadel, a moat, safe rooms of shadow,
'afterwardness' in his thousand yard stare –

years later, decades even, might turn round
to see, through the long tunnel of that gaze,
a yard, a pond and pine trees that surround,
as in a *chaharbagh*, four branching pathways.

Where do memories hide? the pine trees sing.
In language of course, the four pathways reply.
What if the words be lost? the pine trees sigh;

lost, the echo comes, lost like me in air.
Then sing, the pathways answer, sigh and sing
for the echo, for nothing, no one, nowhere.

## MacDONALD DIXON

## Solja

> In loving memory of all those
> who ventured overseas, but
> never returned the way they left.


Clement Welch is a solja in the First West
India regiment, the year is nineteen sixteen,
before we know what it was to be poor: a pair
of second of hand pants, uncertain suppers; empty
stomachs make all of us patriots in the end.

First, is my grandfather, he split for the Isthmus
with half a sovereign in his pocket, dreaming
of a silver mother lode to send back home
for the wife and his struggling brood, still at two.
My mother, the youngest, forget his face as soon
as he climb aboard SS *Chignecto*, bound for
Jamaica then elsewhere unknown to him.

Welch couldn't drink alone no more an' file to fight
for king and country although not quite the right shade.
A band strike up 'There'll ever be an England'
Welch slope arms and march with other recruits, pencil
sharp, not losing a step. My grandfather come back
in a box with his tools, his body somewhere else
rotting; his spar and Viscount Allenby enter
Jerusalem before King and Country dreams turn
sour in his mouth. In France, bewildered, a shovel
was the enemy; shovelling empirical shit.
Shades too black for the trenches, he'd better know his place
and not protest, or else, he'll be shot at dawn
like the rest that hunt for rats with only their shrieks.

Gangrene is a welcome bore, lice and sore-foot
parade in no man's land, waiting for stretchers
to hitch a ride to a hospital cot behind
the lines. That is, until someone enlist us as
cannon fodder for the Turks on another front.

He was good at his tasks and got three stripes
before firing a shot in anger on holy
ground. The stink of empire weaved through his hair,
forgetting who his was, from whence he came. The war
soon over , he came home to a crown grant , tin medals,
and a handshake from his honour that gave him
title to six square chains of mud. He married
a woman from the same place and settled down,
chanting Sancta Lucia every day like prayers
before day break as if not to forget the fortnight
spent in a jail cell at Taranto, Italy,
for firing blanks at god's chosen crew –
it's a crime to be black, he served full time in hell…

BRUCE WEIGL

## The People Have Spoken and They Are Ugly

The people have spoken and they are as ugly as what they don't know. The fascism of populism is now open, and in the air. I wonder what this teaches our children, but I know it's not compassion; it's not love or understanding of others. What will become of them? Make American what again? Make America white again? Make it free of those who dare to cross the borders into light? Soon the free zones will emerge, new borders drawn in whatever blood it will take so those of a kind can flock together beyond what they fear. You know what I mean, this could happen. The people have spoken and they are as ugly as the lies that they told to smother freedom, but you can only change yourself to better understand their greed, you can never change them. This happens in history, this strange swell of ignorance that comes up from some murky place in our hearts when there is a need for blood, and it will last until that need is satisfied. The teacher says: secure the raft of life and death, but it's so hard to act without doing, to walk on the paper thin as air, and never tear a single thread.

## Draft of Final Chorus I

Peace is the new word that you heard, the way of things now. No more hiding in dark bunkers with ghosts who bow to their visitors, come to hide from bombs, their tombs still unprepared in the rice fields. A single new rice plant is laid down. A single new rice plant that could become the world is stuck into the muddy earth so everyone is hurled somehow forward in time, or this may all be a dream that the lost hold onto, so it seems they behold something when they look out across the almost empty fields, they shout to their children who play under a safe sky to come home and eat the little food they have, their eyes resting in a pool of new light, but this is the song of those who fled at the end of days, the helicopters hovering over the embassy like giant insects, the thousands of people fleeing in fear of what they were told, the way they all would die if they stayed, losing track of the incense smoke that could show them their way back home.

## Draft of Final Chorus  II

But there was no slaughter, no crimes against people who left for a country that had come to destroy them, the steeple of the pink cathedral quiet now, only fires burning in the buildings of the failed empire, to keep their secrets buried in the ashes, flashes of the final explosions lighting the sky, this is the song of the people who ran away from their own language, from the spirit kept alive for the thousands of years. They could not stay.  They could not stay when they could ride the hovering helicopters away from some trouble that never would come, so the streets were almost empty for a time, the only sound some joyful celebrations, while the fleet waited at sea for the refugees who gathered around their protectors and guides to a new world as if they were brothers. Who could know how their lives would be, the old flag unfurled in a place so far away. In the snow of America they found their new homes. Or in the warm California sun they laid themselves down in strange beds, the quiet moans of remembering, rising like the mist, like the bells in the pink church that were quiet now.


## War Story

I'm waiting for the war to end for me. I'm waiting for the sound of rockets and mortars to stop rushing through my sleepless nights, for the crack of ambush to quiet, for the movement through the hazy trees to stop and then be nothing but sun coming up through waves of green and yellow bamboo by the river someone had fought hard to defend a thousand years before. I'm waiting for the dead to stop returning from their places in harm's way, so I don't have to care for them anymore. I'm waiting for the war to end for me, the dreams of gun fire out of nowhere, the rounds that I feel in my back going in, the faces of the enemy so near, I can see the oil on their skin. Someone give me something to take or tell me something to believe or teach me something to help forget, but we all know the truth about that now. How there is no way back from the knowing something right down to your soul, how there is no remedy for how the brain is twisted into a loop that will never end, at least this is what they tell us now.

# K. SATCHIDANANDAN

## The Standing Man

A man, still, silent,
stands in the park
where demonstrations
are forbidden.

He is going   nowhere,
nowhere is he coming   from.
The world passes before him
and time, behind him.
In between,
with no flags or slogans,
he stands, still, silent.

The world moves
with the sun.
And he multiplies,
Becomes a hundred,
becomes a thousand.
Hands in pockets,
they just stand, still, silent.

This is a nation in war:
a nation that stands,
stands up against injustice,
a glimpse of the future,
seen in a lightning  flash.

A man stands
in the park,
still, silent,
the sun goes round him.

Poetry is a man
standing alone
in a forbidden space.

# The Kiss

You didn't believe
when the poet said
the world changes
when two people kiss.

See them: a man, a woman,
they kiss.
Not a man and a woman,
but many men, many women.

In the same square where
the enforcers of law
and of morals
used to frown  together
if ever they walked
hand in hand.

A man, a woman,
many men, many women,
in the square,
once a prison to every kiss.

They are breaking the law:
the present's law, of death
they are making the law:
the future's law, of life.

Poetry is a private kiss
provocatively exchanged
in a public space.

*2013*

*translated from the Malayam*

On 17 June 2013, Erdem Gunduz, 34, a choreographer protested against the ban on pro-democracy demonstrations at the Gezi Park in Istanbul by standing still for eight hours: hundreds of people joined him in his non-violent *satyagraha*. And in Turkey's Taksim Square, hundreds of couples protested, by publicly kissing for hours.

**II**

JAMES BERRY

## In God's Greatest Country, 1945

In this Lake Okeechobee land
of hibiscus, oranges and flamingos,
grass could deceive
it was sugarcane.

New like a city boy in
deep woods, I stood inside
the back of the bus, watching
empty seats in front
marked WHITES ONLY.

My friend sat, as any man sits
in a vacant public seat,
and the sun was attacked.
Horns grew in faces.

And the lady squirmed.
She yelled her person's purity
is blotted: a Black
violates her side.

Passions braked the bus.
The driver stood correctly,
legally, holding unholstered gun
coolly, like a Bible
to convert a Black.

'I'm British,' my friend said.
But under steel of eyes
there was a cooler confidence,
'Niggers are jes niggers.'

We stepped down between
fields of nodding sugarcane.

Pop-eyed, at the back of the bus,
with sheep-caged faces,
the black Americans watched us go
across the country road.

In the free sunlight,
satisfying the other tribe,
we walked into the little
segregated town of Belleglade, Florida.


## Travelling As We Are


They hadn't launched their briefing.
They were still cocooned in
the flame of their tongues –
Martin Luther King, Malcolm X,
James Baldwin, etcetera.

My rage unignited
I sat enclosed underground,
British among Britons, only
there, in the nearly empty London
train, going to work.

    Look, Mummy, look, a nigger. Mummy
    niggers can sit here. Mummy, look.

She didn't glance once.
She wouldn't expose a wink.
She withdrew, hooded skilfully
till her southern American voice
trailed a sigh:

    So they can, Tim.
    So they can.

I knew the flight of mind. My
demeaning stressed her excellence,
as I had known it
in her southern US town.

  But this is Europe, Mummy. How come
  niggers live here too?

  Tim and Sally Jane, when you get home
  ask your daddy. You ask your daddy.

Here loaded together we
mattered much to each other,
our tomorrow and yesterday now,
stirring each other, without
a word or glance reciprocated.

An aching hatred left the train
with me. All day suspicion
spurred me. I spoke hastily.
Retaliation wrestled me.

# JOHN AGARD

## Voice

You who even the dumb rejoice in
choreographing with fingers
the miracle of speech
on the parchment of the wind

You who make dreams your element
for the simple reason
that you're on the side
of the tongue's daring to enchant

You who rattle the mouth's gourd
rather than join the dancing
footsteps of the majority
still dancing for their supper

You who make memorable
the poet's word of flesh and bone
distinct from the official Babel
that turns death into collateral

You who set free love's bright syllable
from behind history's iron door
that those who choose to take heed
may stride towards the sky

Viva to you Voice
urging the voiceless to be heard
that even a cry in a wilderness
can ignite the blooming of the world.

# JOY HARJO

## No

Yes that was me you saw shaking with bravery, with a government issued rifle on my back. I'm sorry I could not greet you, as you deserved, my relative.

They were not my tears. I have a reservoir inside. They will be cried by my sons, my daughters if I can't learn how to turn tears to stone.

Yes, that was me standing in the back door of the house in the alley, with fresh corn and bread for the neighbors.

I did not foresee the flood of blood. How they would forget our friendship, would return to kill the babies and me.

Yes, that was me whirling on the dance floor. We made such a racket with all that joy. I loved the whole world in that silly music.

I did not realise the terrible dance in the staccato of bullets.

Yes. I smelled the burning grease of corpses. And like a fool I expected our words might rise up and jam the artillery in the hands of dictators.

We had to keep going. We sang our grief to clean the air of turbulent spirits.

Yes, I did see the terrible black clouds as I cooked dinner. And the messages of the dying spelled there in the ashy sunset. Every one addressed: 'mother'.

There was nothing about it in the news. Everything was the same. Unemployment was up. Another queen crowned with flowers. Then there were the sports scores.

Yes, the distance was great between your country and mine. Yet our children played in the path between our houses.

No. We had no quarrel with each other.

## This Morning I Pray for My Enemies

And whom do I call my enemy?
An enemy must be worthy of engagement.
I turn in the direction of the sun and keep walking.
It's the heart that asks the question, not my furious mind.
The heart is the smaller cousin of the sun.
It sees and knows everything.
It hears the gnashing even as it hears the blessing.
The door to the mind should only open from the heart.
An enemy who gets in, risks the danger of becoming a friend.

# RITA DOVE

## Freedom Ride

As if, after High Street
and the left turn onto Exchange,
the view would veer onto
someplace fresh: Curaçao,
or a mosque adrift on a milk-fed pond.
But there's just more cloud cover,
and germy air
condensing on the tinted glass,
and the little houses with
their fearful patches of yard
rushing into the flames.

Pull the cord a stop too soon, and
you'll find yourself walking
a gauntlet of stares.
Daydream, and you'll wake up
in the stale dark of a cinema,
Dallas playing its mistake over and over
until even that sad reel won't stay
stuck – there's still
Bobby and Malcolm and Memphis,
at every corner the same
scorched brick, darkened windows.

Make no mistake: There's fire
back where you came from, too.
Pick any stop: You can ride
into the afternoon singing with strangers,
or rush home to the scotch
you've been pouring all day –
but where you sit is where you'll be
when the fire hits.

# Teach Us to Number Our Days

In the old neighborhood, each funeral parlor
is more elaborate than the last.
The alleys smell of cops, pistols bumping their thighs,
each chamber steeled with a little blue bullet.

Low rent balconies stacked to the sky.
A boy plays tic-tac-toe on a moon
crossed by TV antennae, dreams

he has swallowed a blue bean.
It takes root in his gut, sprouts
and twines upward, the vines curling
around the sockets and locking them shut.

And this sky, knotted like a dark tie?
The patroller, disinterested, holds all the beans.

August. The mums nod past, each a prickly heart on a sleeve.


# Rosa

How she sat there,
the time right inside a place
so wrong it was ready.

That trim name with
its dream of a bench
to rest on. Her sensible coat.

Doing nothing was the doing:
the clean flame of her gaze
carved by a camera flash.

How she stood up
when they bent down to retrieve
her purse. That courtesy.

PATRICIA SMITH

## How I Won the War

This country wages a savage war inside the blurring borders of my body. I
gulp gorgeous poisons in an attempt to unsettle the soldiers, but they refuse

to cease their incessant bludgeon and scrape. Hoisting their weapons to
threaten my throat, they crash wildly through my ribs, urging me to accept

their generous, just-once offer to lay down arms – but only if I abandon the
thread of Mississippi in my name, scour my skin of shadow and ash, view

myself as they view me. I am screech, belly and head rag. I'm too brash, that
girl who turns landscapes restless and bellows the curious wrongs of mankind,

over and again, I'm just a motto machine. That bothersome blip in my chest is
the cold murmur of the soldiers' cocked rifles. The preacher warned me, so

long ago, that this body – and the shreds of soul clinging to it – might tragically
be the spoil of war. Unless I was Negro wide and aloud, my body was bound

for other hands, for bluster and primp, my exotic womb would be measured to
explain any residual daylight. Preacher, know that every damned day I fight the

faceless regiment inside me, that I'll battle until the night is blown starless,
fight unskirted and dirty, straight through the slow dawn and that midnight

you warned me against. My country seems dead set on draining me of
you. It mocks your softness, says your lessons are ludicrous now that racism

is such a small spot over our shoulders. Dismissing your words as poems and
music, it doesn't know that every single word you uttered was a call to war,

a fervent war with this hated black body as both focus and reward, a war that
wanted my mama's and daddy's Southern names, wanted to straight up slap the

crime of dark deeper into my history. Every day, this war holds up another bright
lie, your words tangled, a fiction I have to surround and shatter to find daybreak.

Preacher, it's true that fewer of us are discovered dangling from the tired arms of trees. But how many brown men were simply grown into the trees, at peace

with their hearts thrumming in the bark? For them, I wish that justice and righteousness came just because it had to, because it was time. Brotherhood

is again a concept, thanks to a white man who struggles comically before he can remember your name. But preacher, I want you to know that I have never

forgotten. I sing you to the reckless soldiers in my body until they become wary of their weapons, until they forget they have sworn to lay waste to a

woman who knows and loves you – not as or in a dream – but as her reality.

# JEAN 'BINTA' BREEZE

## Aid Travels with a Bomb

400 years
from the plantation whip
to the IMF grip

Aid travels with a bomb
Watch out
Aid travels with a bomb

Aid for countries in despair
aid for countries that have no share
they're dumping surplus food in the sea
yet they can't allow starvation to be

They buy your land to dump nuclear waste
you sell it so that food your children can taste

Aid travels with a bomb
Watch out
Aid travels with a bomb

They love your country
they want to invest
but your country don't get
when it come to the test

They rob and exploit you
of your own
then send it back
as a foreign loan
interest is on it
regulations too
they will also decide
your policy for you

Aid travels with a bomb
Watch out
Aid travels with a bomb

They come, they work
they smile so pleased
they leave and you discover
a new disease

Aid travels with a bomb
Watch out
Aid travels with a bomb

You don't know if they're on CIA fee
or even with the KGB
cause you think your country is oh so free
until you look at the economy

Aid travels with a bomb
Watch out!!

# LINTON KWESI JOHNSON

## Reggae Fi Dada

By Galang dada, galang gwwaan yaw sah
Yu nevvah ad no life fi live
Jus' di wan life fi give
Yu did yu time 'pon earth
Yu nevvah get yu jus' dizert
Galang goh smile inna di sun
Galang goh satta inna di palace of peace

Oh di water it so deep
Di water it so dark
An' it full a harbour shark

Di lan' is like a rock
Slowly shattahrin to sun
Sinkin in a sea of calamity
Where fear breed shadows
Dat lurks in di dark
Where people fraid fi walk
Fraid fi tink fraid fi talk
Where di present is haunted by di pass

A deh so mi bawn
Get fi know 'bout staam
Learn fi cling to di dawn
An' wen mi hear mi daddy sick
Mi quickly pack an' tek a trip

Mi nevvah have no time when mi reach
Fi si no sunny beach wen mi reach
Jus' people a live in shack
People livin back-to-back
Mongst cackroach an' rat
Mongst dirt an' disease
Subjec to terrorist attack
Political intrigue, constant grief
An' no sign of relief

Oh di grass turn brown
So many trees cut doun
An' di lan' is ovahgrown
From country to town
Is jus' tissel an' tawn
Inna di woun a di poor
Is a miracle ow dem endure

Di pain nite an' day
Di stench of decay
Di clarin' sights
Di guarded affluence
Di arrogant vices
Cole eyes of kantemp
Di mackin' symbols of independence

A deh so mi bawn
Get fi know 'bout staam
Learn fi cling to di dawn
An' wen di news reach mi
Seh mi wan daddy ded
Mi ketch a plane quick

An' wen mi reach mi sunny isle
It was di same ole style
Di money well dry
Di bullits dem a fly
Plenty innocent a die
Many rivers run dry
Ganja planes flyin' high
Di poor man him a try
Yu tink a lickle try him try
Holdin' awn bye an' bye
Wen a dallah cyaan buy
A lickle dinnah fi a fly

Galang dada, galang gwwaan yaw sah
Yu nevvah ad no life fi live
Jus' di wan life fi give
Yu did yu time 'pon earth
Yu nevvah get yu jus' dizert

Galang goh smile inna di sun
Galang goh satta inna di palace of peace

Mi know yu couldn't tek it dada
Di anguish an' di pain
Di suffahrin' di problems di strain
Di strugglin' in vain
Fi mek two ens meet
So dat dem pickney coulda get
A lickle someting fi eat
Fi put cloths 'pon dem back
Fi put shoes 'pon dem feet
Wen a dallah cyaan buy
A lickle dinnah fi a fly

Mi know yu try dada
Yu fight a good fight
But di dice dem did loaded
An' di card pack fix
Yet still yu reach fifty-six
Before yu lose yu leg wicket
'A no yu bawn grung here'
So wi bury yu a Stranger's Burying Groun
Near to mhum an' cousin Daris
Not far fram di quarry doun a August Town

## BASHABI FRASER


## To Martin Luther King: Neal Hall in Kolkata


I heard your compatriot recall 9/11
To commemorate his communities' 24/7
For those forcibly dragged to the land of liberty
To endure the darkest captivity with dignity.

I witnessed his angst, not at the perpetrators
Enacting laws to isolate, denigrate, segregate
The sowers, reapers and architects of land and city
Who have existed in a sizzling crater.

He addressed the silent ones whose compassion
Is not enough, those who are afraid to protest
As a whole race is cornered into oblivion
In a country which has dreams for the rest

But not for those it forcibly brought to its shores.
He spoke about Dachau repeated in your land
A holocaust willed on your strand
Flogged, lynched, bulleted or imprisoned.

Today he stands with glowing pride
In what was the second city of Empire
A poet who today rides
The wind of your dreams and desires.

# Freedom's Call

You met me in my day of success
When I sang to celebrate my freedom
Of flight across a boundless sky

I was at the treetop height of bliss
When you captured me from my skydom
Chained me and forbid me to fly.

Today I sit in your gilded cage
My wings are static by my side
I survive on fragments you throw here

My endless joy has turned to rage
My urge to fly does not subside
I feel a surging wave of fear

Sweep through my frozen little frame
It flows with intent through this lair
It shoots like arrows through these bars

It startles you like summer rain
A song that challenges and dares
The rising wind and the distant star.

So I will sing to freedom's call
I will dream of trees ablaze
With colours that the molten sun

Has decreed to one and all.

# NIKKY FINNEY

## Red Velvet

*(for Rosa Parks, 1913–2005)*

> People always say that I didn't give up my seat because I was tired, but that
> isn't true. I was not tired physically, or no more tired than I usually was at
> the end of a working day. No – the only thing I was – was tired of giving in.
>
> ROSA PARKS

I

*Montgomery, Alabama, 1955*

*The setting*: A rolling box with wheels
*The players:* Mr Joe Singleton, Rev. Scott,
       Miss Louise Bennett, Mrs Rosa Parks,
       Jacob & Junie (fraternal twins, fourteen)

*The game:* Pay your Indian Head to the driver,
   then get off the bus.
   Then, walk to the door at the end of the bus.
   Then, reboard the bus through the Black back door.
   (Then, push *repeat* for fifty years.)

Sometimes, the driver pulled off,
before the paid-in-full customer
could get to the one open door.

Fed up with buses driving off – without them –
just as her foot lifted up, grazing, the steel step:

She was not a child. She was in her forties.
A seamstress. A woman devoted to
handmade things.

She had grown up in a place:
where only white people had power,
where only white people passed good jobs on
      to other white people,

where only white people loaned money
        to other white people,
where only white people were considered human
        by other white people,
where only the children of white people had new
        books on the first day of school,
where only white people could drive to the store
        at midnight for milk
        (without having to watch the rearview).

## II

A seamstress brings fabric and thread, collars & hems,
buttonholes, together. She is one who knows her way
around velvet.

Arching herself over a river of cloth she feels for the bias,
but doesn't cut, not until the straight pins are in place,
marking everything; in time, everything will come together.

Nine months after, December 1, 1955, Claudette
Colvin, fifteen, arrested for keeping her seat; before that,
Mary Louise Smith. The time to act, held by two pins.

## III

The Montgomery seamstress waits and waits for
the Cleveland Avenue bus. She climbs aboard,
row five. The fifth row is the first row of the Colored
section. The bus driver, who tried to put her off that day,
had put her off twelve years before. But twelve years
before she was only twenty-eight, still a child to the
heavy work of resistance.

By forty-two, you have pieced & sewn many things
together in segregated Alabama. You have heard
'Nigger Gal' more times than you can stitch your
manners down. You have smelled fear cut through
the air like sulfur iron from the paper mills. The pants,
shirts, and socks that you have darned perfectly, routinely,
walk perfectly, routinely, by you. (*Afternoon. How do.*)
Those moving along so snug in your well-made, well-sewn
clothes, spit routinely, narrowly missing your perfectly
pressed sleeve.

By forty-two, your biases are flat, your seams are inter-
locked, your patience with fools, razor thin.

By forty-two, your heart is heavy with slavery, lynching,
and the lessons of being 'good'. You have heard
7,844 Sunday sermons on how God made every
woman in his image. You do a lot of thinking with
a thimble on your thumb. You have hemmed
8,230 skirts for nice, well-meaning, white women
in Montgomery. You have let the hem out of
18,809 pant legs for growing white boys. You have
pricked your finger 45,203 times. Held your peace.

#### IV

December 1, 1955: You didn't notice who was
driving the bus. Not until you got on. Later you
would remember, 'All I wanted was to get home.'
The bus driver, who put you off when you were
twenty-eight, would never be given the pleasure
of putting you off anything ever again. When he
asks you to move you cross your feet at the ankle.

*Well    I'm going to have you arrested.*

And you, you with your forty-two years, with your
21,199 perfect zippers, you with your beautiful
nation of perfect seams marching all in place, all
around Montgomery, Alabama, on the backs &
hips of Black & white alike, answer him back,

*Well – You may go on and do so.*

You are arrested on a Thursday. That night in
Montgomery, Dr King led the chant, 'There
comes a time when people just get tired.' (He
wasn't quite right, but he was King.) He asked
you to stand so your people can see you. You
stand. *Veritas!* You do not speak. The indelible
blue ink still on your thumb saying, *Enough!*
You think about the qualities of velvet: strength
& sway. How mighty it holds the thread and

won't let go. You pull your purse in close,
the blue lights map out your thumb, blazing
the dark auditorium.

On Courthouse Monday, the sun day dew
sweating the grass, you walk up the sidewalk
in a long-sleeved black dress, your white collar
and deep perfect cuffs holding you high and
starched in the Alabama air. A trim black velvet
hat, a gray coat, white gloves. You hold your
purse close: everything valuable is kept near
the belly, just like you had seen your own mother
do. You are pristine. Persnickety. Particular.
A seamstress. Every thing about you gathered
up and in place. A girl in the crowd, taught not to
shout, shouts, 'Oh! She's so sweet looking! Oh!
They done messed with the wrong one now.'

You cannot keep messing with a sweet-looking
Black woman who knows her way around velvet.
A woman who can take cotton and gabardine,
seersucker and silk, swirl tapestry, and hang
boiled wool for the house curtains, to the very
millimeter. A woman made of all this is never to
be taken for granted, never to be asked to move
to the back of anything, never ever to be arrested.

A woman who believes she is worthy of every
thing possible. Godly. Grace. Good. Whether you
believe it or not, she has not come to Earth to play
Ring Around Your Rosie on your rolling
circus game of public transportation.

A woman who understands the simplicity pattern,
who wears a circle bracelet of straight pins there,
on the tiny bend of her wrist. A nimble, on-the-dot
woman, who has the help of all things, needle sharp,
silver, dedicated, electric, can pull cloth and others
her way, through the tiny openings she and others
before her have made.

A fastened woman
can be messed with, one too many times.

With straight pins poised in the corner
of her slightly parted lips, waiting to mark
the stitch, her fingers tacking,
looping the blood red wale,

through her softly clenched teeth
she will tell you, without ever looking
your way,

*You do what you need to do &*
*So will I.*


## My Time Up with You

*[A rickety porch somewhere in east Texas,]*

          the     air     is     calamity

The TV camera steadies against the wind, shining
the only good light left on the old woman's face.

    *Ain't going nowhere. Ain't moving. Not from this house.*

The young man does not drop head or microphone.

    *Go save somebody else. Everybody at 621 already saved.*

With her cane she points to the bright orange house numbers.
The young reporter does not speak. The sheriff deputy's
face is ruddy, puffing. He is nearly eating his car radio;

    *We ARE trying to get out. Roger, we are trying to get out now! Over.*

The young 'tom brokaw' situates the camera on her face.
Mayree Monroe is chewing down an old bone, taken out
of her mama's mouth. A bone that won't go down.

*You say Rita coming? Well, she just gonna have to come on.*

Miss Monroe hands the sky everything in her pockets.

*Come on Rita girl. Come on gal, get yourself on Mayree's list.*

Her eyes & words fall to Mr. Tall Handsome, camera-
keeping up with her every move;

*Iss gonna be me and Rita tonight, Baby!*

He hoists the great silver eye off his shoulder. Looking
behind, on guard to the loud laughing wind. No time.
He's got to make her understand.

One hour ago when they arrived for this little
human-interest story, he didn't think it would
take this long. How could it take this long? All
up and down the street: Whipping clotheslines.
Spanking trash cans. Snapping live wires.
Twenty-foot vaulted trees. Downspouts playing
steel pan with the trembling ground. Every wild
thing prone to stillness now. Miss Monroe's screen
cracks then pops. The top hinge lunges wild, free.

*Miss Monroe, please come with us, everybody has been
evacuated – but you. We need to get in the car now and go.
We really need to go. If we leave without you no one will
come back for you – not even when you change your mind.*

He means well. He has a kind voice. Wearing
those You Can Trust Me I Served In The Peace
Corps eyes. He has seen the inside of a church
twice, walking all the way to the front both
times, surprising even his mother as he dropped
to his knees.

The old woman, three times his age, points, then
claps her hands like a much younger woman.
When she does her top teeth shift, slip. She stands.
Using both hands she smooths down the cotton

fabric from hipline to another invisible mark just
above her knee. She does this in one fluid motion.
This is the oldest signal in the Western Hemisphere
between an old Black woman and whosoever
her company happens to be.

*My time up with you* her standing-up legs and
smoothing-down hand signals say. But the young
'tom brokaw' has not studied his field guide
to Black women.

With help of the feral wind Mayree Monroe comes
to her highest height. He continues to pan & zoom,
finding the strip of duct tape holding crooked the
one arm of her black-rimmed glasses. She kisses
her fingers then waves to his curvy green glass third
eye. Imitating the long-legged Black girls from the
Ebony Fashion Fair, found in her monthly *JET*
magazine, she arcs her thin arms toward the giant
orange 621, newly painted and still drying on the
front of her house. Before the deputy arrived,
while Oakland Road piled into SUVs & flatbeds,
with engines still running, Mayree Monroe hunted
for her paintbrush.

She turns and walks inside her shotgun house,
pushing and latching the screen door so hard
until the picture of her wavy blond Redeemer
goes wavy – shakes, but does not fall. The camera
keeps churning. The old woman starts her roll
call, using her fingers to count. The patrol lights
on the Sheriff's car twirl in front like the vehicle
that has come to escort a person of importance
to the County Fair, where once in their seats,
all will hear the cigar-laced midget ring out:

*Come and See the Disappearing Lady!*
*Here one minute gone the next!*

*I told you*, the deputy says to 'tom brokaw',
*'hit was the same as this morning. She named*

*every last one she's lived through.* David '79.
Charley '80. Norma '81. *She give the name and*
*the year perfect.* Bonnie '86. Gilbert '88. Arlene '93.
Bret '99. Claudette '03. *Name and year, one by one.*

The young 'tom brokaw' zooms in and frames
the 621. He quickly brings the camera down.
The engine is running. Mayree Monroe has shut
her door in his face. Both of the deputy's feet
are in the car tapping the sopping floor mats.
Boards and metal siding fly then tumble down
the street. Young 'tom brokaw' does not turn
his back to her. His eyes flutter, up and around
every missing nail and dangling soffit in sight.
For the third time in his life he is back on his
knees. He backs his way to the car lowering his
camera to the seat. His cheeks are not as dry
as the skittish lawman's. He slides his boots in,
his body fights his mind & knees – then follows.

The Texas dust is laid down.

Through the thin laminated door he hears
Mayree Monroe latching her three deadbolts.
The two-by-four that her nephew, Jimmy, cut &
nailed for added protection, is squeezed down
& over iron brackets bolted into the wall.
It is the same as any other night. Alone, finally,
with her wavy-haired Redeemer.

> *Master of Man, where they gonna send Mayree Monroe?*
> *I already got me a house. What's a Superdome anyway?*
> *What kind of a name is U-tah? U-tah don't sound nice*
> *as Texarkana. Rent free, they quick to say.*

She shakes her fist. The blinding rain is now flooding
every street for thirty miles in every direction. All phone
lines are down now. Lights, out now. She searches a
wooden drawer for a match to light her grandmother's
cobalt blue kerosene lamp.

*Never give me nothing free before. Now all of a sudden*
*they handing out Free! like butter or jumbo packs of Juicy*
*Fruit. Sweet Redeemer, where does Mayree go when she has*
*finally paid off her house and the mannish hurricane is*
*thundering down?*

Mayree Monroe's hand is steady. She strikes her one
piney match in one praising stroke. The room blooms
around her with the shadows of her precious things.
A zephyr hits the porch so hard a marble hole happens
quick to the wall. She does not look.

> *I have paid off this house three times over what anybody*
> *else ever would've paid. Nobody at Community Savings*
> *& Trust thought I could do it.*

> *Just like nobody in that yard today believe I can make it*
> *through this night. Disbelief will run you straight into*
> *the arms of the Devil. My Sweet Redeemer.*

> *Lily of my Valley, 'odds ain't the best' they say. Did you*
> *hear 'em talkin' to me that way?*

Dropping her voice down to a whisper, she stands like a
black beam against the wind, both arms akimbo.

> *Well, odds ain't never been the best*
> *for Mayree Monroe and her kind.*

Walking over to her rocker, she pulls the thin cushion
off the seat, weaving left arm over right arm, she straps
in for the night.

> *'Change my mind?' 'tom brokaw' have the nerve to*
> *shape his mouth and say. This Mayree Monroe,*
> *of 621 Oakland Avenue, daughter of Ester Brown,*
> *of 18 Clementine Road, granddaughter of Mary One,*
> *of Route 4, Box 318. I will be here till the end.*

69

# E. ETHELBERT MILLER

## The Last Ritual

We need to wash our bowls.
Place them in the sun.

Ah – the belly is filled with joy.
No more hunger for Peace.

MONIZA ALVI

## I Hold My Breath in This Country with Its Sad Past

I hold my breath for fear of saying the wrong thing.

I hold my breath in admiration.

Because everything points to this hinterland –
the generosity of the people
the rawness of the cold
the over-heated rooms
the scooped-out cottage-loaf filled with soup.

And sometimes all talk seems delicately
configured around a silence.

I can't begin to imagine how a whole people
could be so cruelly punished.

Slowly, slowly the present
slips through the hands of the past.
And at the flick of a switch

it is red and not grey that I see
beneath the thin layer of snow.

Up the main street, under the Christmas lights
stalk the wolves, lynxes and brown bears
of the forests, and even they
have thoughts, sorrow and pride.

## How the Children Were Born

Doctors and midwives were aghast.
There, embedded in each infant palm
was the barrel of a tiny gun.

Babies had always raged – but
could any child be born knowing,
and prepared for war?

Enmity was handed down
like an heirloom.
The guns grew with the babies,
poking like bone through the soft skin.


## How the Stone Found Its Voice

We had waited through so many lifetimes
for the stone to speak, wondered if

it would make compelling pronouncements,
anything worth writing down.

Then after the war of wars
had ground to a shattering halt, the stone

emitted a small grinding sound rather like
the clearing of a throat.

Let us be indifferent to indifference,
the stone said.

And then the world spoke.

## BENJAMIN ZEPHANIAH

## I Have a Scheme

I am here today my friends to tell you there is hope
As high as that mountain may seem
I must tell you
I have a dream
And my friends
There is a tunnel at the end of the light.
And beyond that tunnel I see a future
I see a time
When angry white men
Will sit down with angry black women
And talk about the weather,
Black employers will display notice-boards proclaiming,
'Me nu care wea yu come from yu know
So long as yu can do a good day's work, dat cool wid me.'

I see a time
When words like affirmative action
Will have sexual connotations
And black people all over this blessed country of ours
Will play golf,
Yes my friends that time is coming
And in that time
Afro-Caribbean and Asian youth
Will spend big money on English takeaways
And all police officers will be armed
With a dumplin,
I see a time
A time when the President of the United States of America will stand up and say,
'I inhaled
And it did kinda nice
So rewind and cum again.'
Immigration officers will just check that you are all right
And all black people will speak Welsh.

I may not get there my friends
But I have seen that time
I see thousands of muscular black men on Hampstead Heath walking their
     poodles
And hundreds of black female Formula 1 drivers
Racing around Birmingham in pursuit of a truly British way of life.
I have a dream
That one day from all the churches of this land we will hear the sound of that
     great old English spiritual,
*Here we go, Here we go, Here we go.*
One day all great songs will be made that way.

I am here today my friends to tell you
That the time is coming
When all people, regardless of gender, colour or class, will have at least one
     Barry Manilow record
And vending-machines throughout the continent of Europe
Will flow with sour sap and sugarcane juice,
For it is written in the great book of multiculturalism
That the curry will blend with the shepherd's pie
And the Afro hairstyle will return.

Let me hear you say
Multiculture
Amen
Let me hear you say
Roti, Roti
A women.

The time is coming
I may not get there with you
But I have seen that time,
And as an Equal Opportunities poet
It pleases me
To give you this opportunity
To share my vision of hope
And I just hope you can cope
With a future as black as this.

## GRACE NICHOLS

## A Brief Odyssey

The toddler whose body was laughter
happy even after they had to flee
the grey rubble of what was once home.

A live-wire, all jumps and chants,
he repeated the words of his father –
*Eu-rope, boat-trip, new-home-new-home.*

Dressed as if for an outing, a great adventure,
he, his brother and anxious parents,
all headed for the Aegean – Homer's mythic sea –

*But the night it was dark*
*and the sea it was uncalm*
*and the boat – an over-crowded dingy –*
*set sail like a gamble against an hourglass.*

Ill wind, ill fated odyssey –
leaving only a father to tell
the dazed tale of how they all slipped –
his clinging fingers turned to sand –

The live-wire, all jumps and chants,
returned by the abiding manes of the sea –
a small and casual sacrifice
on the shore of Poseidon's omnivorous heart.

# KENDAL HIPPOLYTE

## Poem in a manger

where is the poem?
not on this page i'm looking at and reading from
where is the poem?
not here, not in these miserable words i'm writing now,
though i have to write them, though you have to
read them, see them, hear them

cause really, if i could, i'd make this page
howl at you, the paper burn crisp, the letters burst
like pustules and pressurised blood vessels, so you would see
on opening this inadequate irrelevant book
flipping this ridiculous bit of paper
not a poem
but a baby blackening and charred and smoking still
cindered by its private holocaust-to-come.

if this baby
would curl and stretch and stiffen
one last time like a burnt page in a still wind
if this baby
would show its blackening sooty teeth
like letters hitting a page
without a        w        o        r        d
if it would turn over on its back
contracting to a bitter foetus, regretting every screaming
moment it was in the blank book of the living
if you'd see this
hear this, touch the wincing flesh of it
just as you turned this page
if you'd see – goddam it, why don't you! –
that the baby on this page, disguised as a raving poem
is you, really all the time is you

then how
would there ever be again another war
another flash of nitroglycerine
another tin soldier flashing tin-medalled teeth
another jack-booted 'yes-i'm-ready' puppet in the box
another and another and another and another
wall-eyed uniformed somebody's son to press or pull or push or ram
the triggers, switches, levers, plungers, pins, paraphernalia of the
weltering world-waste of another war?

how would there be
if this baby, swaddled in words, lying on this inadequate page
would burn alive
before your eyes and howling all the time
that it was you?

if you would see, then you'd see why
the poem isn't on this fucking page
then you'd see where the poem has gone
and why i'm trying to use these useless goddam
words to catch it, and
why i need you to
help me do that

look at the page again:
these are just words

let us go find the poem

## CARL PHILLIPS

## Haloing the Lion

It had seemed a good thing. And if from the beginning
there'd been also a certain sense of – well, doom
frankly, can we be blamed, given our lives, for
assuming doom as, if not the key part, then
an essential part of it: as in, without doom
how would good have had a shot at all at becoming
knowable? Who among us didn't understand at least
about that? They say faithless and unfaithful
are not the same. Go figure. As if some kind of truce
or non-truce faded ages ago
had ever been the subject. This much I'll swear to:
it was dark, mostly; we lived just west of here,
beside a sea into which the twin stars Detachment
and Obedience are said to have fallen and, ever since,
keep smoldering – the water's that warm, the waves themselves,
when they break, sing with it, *What's a halo to a lion, anyway*, forever.

# IMTIAZ DHARKER

## Looking away from Lucky Boy

Welcome milk-and-honey cup has soured
to poison, open arms turned prison,
freedom map has lost its roads.

This place. I swallowed its stars
and spangles, knew its passwords and its codes.
They called me Lucky, Lucky Boy, but now

my luck has flown away. You hold the torch
up high, just to scorch the thing I was.
I came across black water to reach you,

and you are watching your phone
while I drown.

I caught your sun in a cup of faith and drank it,
danced in love and dreamed beneath your moon.
I knew your songs by heart and lived them

because I would rise, I would fly
on lucky wings. They called me Lucky,
Lucky Boy until it changed.

You turned your face away from me
and my burning wings. I am looking
back at you. You are on your phone

and don't look round,
not even to watch as I go down.

# MARTÍN ESPADA

## How We Could Have Lived or Died This Way

> Not songs of loyalty alone are these,
> But songs of insurrection also,
> For I am the sworn poet of every dauntless rebel the world over.
>
> WALT WHITMAN

I see the dark-skinned bodies falling in the street as their ancestors fell
before the whip and steel, the last blood pooling, the last breath spitting.
I see the immigrant street vendor flashing his wallet to the cops,
shot so many times there are bullet holes in the soles of his feet.
I see the deaf woodcarver and his pocketknife, crossing the street
in front of a cop who yells, then fires. I see the drug raid, the wrong
door kicked in, the minister's heart seizing up. I see the man hawking
a fistful of cigarettes, the cop's chokehold that makes his wheezing
lungs stop wheezing forever. I am in the crowd, at the window,
kneeling beside the body left on the asphalt for hours, covered in a sheet.

I see the suicides: the conga player handcuffed for drumming on the subway,
hanged in the jail cell with his hands cuffed behind him; the suspect leaking
blood from his chest in the back seat of the squad car; the 300-pound boy
said to stampede barehanded into the bullets drilling his forehead.

I see the coroner nodding, the words he types in his report burrowing
into the skin like more bullets. I see the government investigations stacking,
words buzzing on the page, then suffocated as bees suffocate in a jar. I see
the next Black man, fleeing as the fugitive slave once fled the slave-catcher,
shot in the back for a broken tail light. I see the cop handcuff the corpse.

I see the rebels marching, hands upraised before the riot squads,
faces in bandannas against the tear gas, and I walk beside them unseen.
I see the poets, who will write the songs of insurrection generations unborn
will read or hear a century from now, words that make them wonder
how we could have lived or died this way, how the descendants of slaves
still fled and the descendants of slave-catchers still shot them, how we awoke
every morning without the blood of the dead sweating from every pore.

# Sleeping on the Bus

How we drift in the twilight of bus stations,
how we shrink in overcoats as we sit,
how we wait for the loudspeaker
to tell us when the bus is leaving,
how we bang on soda machines
for lost silver, how bewildered we are
at the vision of our own faces
in white-lit bathroom mirrors.

How we forget the bus stations of Alabama,
Birmingham to Montgomery,
how the Freedom Riders were abandoned
to the beckoning mob, how afterwards
their faces were tender and lopsided as spoiled fruit,
fingers searching the mouth for lost teeth,
and how the riders, descendants
of Africa and Europe both, kept riding
even as the mob with pleading hands wept fiercely
for the ancient laws of segregation.

How we forget Biloxi, Mississippi, a decade before,
where no witnesses spoke to cameras,
how a brown man in military uniform
was pulled from the bus by police
when he sneered at the custom of the back seat,
how the magistrate proclaimed a week in jail
and went back to bed with a shot of whiskey,
how the brownskinned soldier could not sleep
as he listened for the prowling of his jailers,
the muttering and cardplaying of the hangmen
they might become.
His name is not in the index;
he did not tell his family for years.
How he told me, and still I forget.

How we doze upright on buses,
how the night overtakes us
in the babble of headphones,

how the singing and clapping
of another generation
fade like distant radio
as we ride, forehead
heavy on the window,
how we sleep, how we sleep.


## Litany at the Tomb of Frederick Douglass

*Mount Hope Cemetery, Rochester, New York, November 7, 2008*


This is the longitude and latitude of the impossible;
this is the epicenter of the unthinkable;
this is the crossroads of the unimaginable:
the tomb of Frederick Douglass, three days after the election.

This is a world spinning away from the gravity of centuries,
where the grave of a fugitive slave has become an altar.
This is the tomb of a man born as chattel, who taught himself to read in secret,
scraping the letters in his name with chalk on wood; now on the anvil-flat stone
a campaign button fills the O in *Douglass*. The button says: *Obama*.
This is the tomb of a man in chains, who left his fingerprints
on the slavebreaker's throat so the whip would never carve his back again;
now a labor union T-shirt drapes itself across the stone, offered up
by a nurse, a janitor, a bus driver. A sticker on the sleeve says: *I Voted Today*.
This is the tomb of a man who rolled his call to arms off the press,
peering through spectacles at the abolitionist headline; now a newspaper
spreads above his dates of birth and death. The headline says: *Obama Wins*.

This is the stillness at the heart of the storm that began in the body
of the first slave, dragged aboard the first ship to America. Yellow leaves
descend in waves, and the newspaper flutters on the tomb, like the sails
Douglass saw in the bay, like the eyes of a slave closing to watch himself
escape with the tide. Believers in spirits would see the pages trembling
on the stone and say: look how the slave boy teaches himself to read.
I say a prayer, the first in years: that here we bury what we call
the impossible, the unthinkable, the unimaginable, now and forever. *Amen.*

# CORNELIUS EADY

## Emmett Till's Glass Top Casket

By the time they cracked me open again, topside, abandoned in a toolshed, I had become another kind of nest. Not many people connect possums with Chicago,

but this is where the city ends, after all, and I float still, after the footfalls fade and the roots bloom around us. The fact was, everything that worked for my young man

worked for my new tenants. The fact was, he had been gone for years. They lifted him from my embrace, and I was empty, ready. That's how the possums found me, friend,

dry-docked, a tattered mercy hull. Once I held a boy who didn't look like a boy. When they finally remembered, they peeked through my clear top. Then their wild surprise.

## Future Crimes

> if a man is constantly guilty
> for what goes on in his mind
> give me the electric chair
> for all my future crimes...
>
> PRINCE

I am guilty.
I am cop guilty.
I am MERCEDES guilty.
I am shoot you in the back guilty.
I know I am guilty
For what goes on in my mind.

I know I am guilty
When the cop pulls me over.
I know he knows I am guilty.
So these bullets in my back
As I try running,
So this lead tattoo
Against my shirt:
– I had this coming.
– I took a ride, love.
This crime of passion
That sets me free,
That sets me free,
I am constantly guilty
For what goes on in his mind,
The mind of this cop,
Who knows if he doesn't stop me now,
My loose black body in the world...
I know who you are, says the cop,
And it's not mistaken identity,
Because we know I am guilty
For all my future crimes,
For all my future crimes.
This is me, chosen, turning on
My heels,
My weird, half broken gallop,
Wishing for wings, wishing for lift
Wishing for luck, wishing for bad aim, or
A shell, spent just before the target is kissed.
This is me, selected, my black back running
Out of the life I thought I had,
Out of the simple boredom of the day.
Sooner or later, my breathing kin,
This is simply what goes on.

*for Walter Scott*

## The Blues

What are these songs we Negro sing, these wee, woe strums,
Compared to the naked fists
I see, roaming the street, seeking skin
To knuckle open, their hunger to be a jive magnet,
Chaos, hammering a skull.

*

When the housecat shakes the vole in its jaws
And out rises that last blue squeal? That note,
And all the misery before it, the freedom
To gaze and choose and snatch without reproach.

*

Oh Lord, oh Lord, oh Lordy-Lord.

*

They ache to blister us.

*

Go ahead and read them the law.
That's the sound of their blues
In that barb-wired heaven.

# BERNARDINE EVARISTO

## The Lexical Rebellion of Protest

I

& suddenly it was the era of post-*rahtid*-rassism
globally loud-haloed by the amassedwhitemedia
upon the enstoolment of the first black president of the us of a

glassceiling smashed
job done
we are all one
pax!

(majorfail of magic-wandery bollocks, actually)

II

the illusionaryinclusionary of britannia's centurions
multi-culti advertisements/ receptionists/ televisionpresenters
the publicfaceof – marketing the nation

frustrating our vox melanoidinal demographicalrage

while persons ofinfluence whitegaze
inequalities conveniently viewed at othercountry distance
always overthere/ overthere/ overthere

one's moral-opprobrium is morally-unimpeachable
when it's overthere

III

ourown    c(o)vert-discrimination & unconscious-bias (PLU)
          impoverishment/socialhousing/ lowerpayscales
          defacto debarment from the directorate of the hegemon
          tokenised&isolated presence in the whitecollar workforce
          gross mis-management (of expectation) at all levels

ourown  metropoliced cities (IC1) versus incarcerated males (IC3)
     racialprofiling versus positiverolemodelling
     guilty of walkingwhileblack & hunted down mini-mart aisles
     3 x harsher sentences/ 3 x exclusion from schools
     macro (psychological) impact of micro (passive) aggressions

ourown  absentfather sons & strongbacksingle females
     lackof communitycohesion-ism & pulltheladderup-ism
     time keeping/ BPT/ soon come o'clock/ is nojoke
     lack of collective activism towards activating c.h.a.n.g.e
     (while riots do not a revolution make – in Tottenham)


### IV

we're still living with imperialism's mindfuck legacy
colonialideology underclassing afro-british citizenry
subjugate/sub-ordinate/subalternate
in conformance with the subjectivities of the race-coded
obsessions of the tribalmajority
(who profess to be colourblind)
our i.d. (not id)
always
identifiable
by our figurative *couleur noir*
our faces pre-conceptually processed
our afro-concentrics of thick helix hair
hotironcombed
or not


### V

WTFdowedo when we are but 0.49% of the professoriate – flying solo?
WTFhappens to the conversation & promulgation of knowledgeispower?
*whose* history/ politics/ law/ health/ arts/ business/ STEM?
*whose* priorities/opinions/ policies/ research/ think-tanks/punditry?
WTFhappens to the youngsters coming up/ reflection-less/ rudder-less
who will speak for us when *we* are not there to speak for us?

## VI

thank goodness social media's online communications
are beyondborders & timelines & uncensored by the keepers of the gate

> #decolonisingtheacademy
> #blacklivesmatter (as well)
> #intersectionality
> #everydaysexism
> #bornthiswaylgbtq
> #speaktruthtopower
> #whiteprivilege (checkit)
> #whitetears (checkit)

## VII

today is the let's make Britain great again shitstirring of mimicmen
bringing out our worstselves/ demagogues@hate.co.uk #1933
scapegoating scumbags spewforthing xenophobic          bile
blaming the immigrants who brought *everybody* here

## VIII

for we are the alwayswas, everhere, evermore & everywhere
wayback to firsthumanoid roaming to find shelterfoodhome

## IX

meanwhile, the superich sail off into taxhaven sunsets on superyachts

## X

today is                    unfinished business

                                        roar

## IAN DUHIG

## Croix-des-Bouquets, Haiti

Most were naked but for the locked tin masks
which stop them sucking the cane they harvest.
We could see they had been made tigerish

by their whippings. Our sabres stuck in bone,
our saddle-girths were slashed by their children,
crones tore shot from the mouths of primed cannon

while our powder-monkeys fumbled and wept.
But we have laid them up in lavender.
They think their dead will wake in Africa.

## Fatras Baton

The sugar falls like black snow on Noé
by where Mackandal the Poisoner
was burnt and burst from his stake.

Napoleon's new Commissioner,
the insane Sonthonax, is white
yet incites d'occos to slaughter whites.

Our Black Spartacus, l'Ouverture,
protects us, but grows smoky-haired with age.
(Napoleon has marked him for exile).

The English say we French must like burnt sugar
in our coffee. I toast their officers
from our very best Jacobite glass.

My darling, I write under a bad turn of the moon.
Kiss the children for me. If I should not return
claim compensation. Burn the punishment books.

# TIM SEIBLES

## Ghost

> I may not get there with you, but I want you to know tonight that we, as a people, will get to the Promised Land.
>
> MLK, Jr

Do you remember
that unchecked faith? –
the world itself, a promise:
a child, you dream something
and it glistens. You wake up
and can't believe it
isn't there.

In '63, the country
seemed ready to begin
a future tinted with love
or, at least, singed
by a genuine disdain
for injustice. Washington, DC.
The White House built
by slaves. The March.

Me    standing in Lincoln's
shadow. I really believed
there was something
I could say. All those faces –
black *and* white – wanting
my words to unchain the future.

I was never naïve enough
to think the *dream* would not
require blood – surely
Malcolm's    and probably
my own. I *did* hope to live
a long life, but always
figured I might be undone

by stupidity – its array
of daily faces and
perfectly pressed uniforms.
Even heading to Selma,
seeing those troopers
across the bridge, it took
all I had not to holler

*Who are we kidding? These fools*
*will never change.*
Cruelty does as much work
on the cruel    as on their
victims – the way, for example,
wrong-headed power learns
to love itself: just ask
The Ku Klux. Ask anybody
besieged by a system guaranteed
to kill them slowly: the real violence

is *just business* – cool handshakes
between suits, no money
for schools, smirks between
badges while the churches
burn. I mean

what part of this    *don't you*
understand?  Frederick Douglass
already said what I was trying to say.
He had a dream a hundred years
before I did, but nobody shot him
(and his second wife was white!)
Some days, you just have to laugh.

Despite Obama, certain trees
still hold their congress    though most
of the men and women who fed
those mobs are long gone to dust.
But the ropes remain

tying our hands, stopping
our throats. Hard to say what

'faith in democracy' means now –
look who you just elected.

What exactly would you
have me say? *We shall*

*overcome?* That sniper
has already seen my neck,
marched me right

into history     at last.
I'll never be more

free     than this

III

# FRED D'AGUIAR

## Call & Response

1

Dear Martin, I wish you had never been found.
Telescope and direction, aim, hammer, grudge,
Velocity and malice sent me, your bloodhound.
As I burned through space, left my own sound
In my wake, parted strands from my site, dodged
Time, split particles, my Hummingbird instant
For your slow, finger wet in mouth test of falling,
Swept aside by my speed inside your constant,
I knew where I would end up, what my blunt
Instrument must do to your routine, more calling
Than career, to that bigger dream you coined,
Robbed of you, grabbed by me, us joined.

I knew others would follow you in my name,
For no other reason than that my trade is grief,
I bear harm, win nothing, end warmth, halt fame.
I flew to you knowing violence would be blamed,
Not me, I saw all the things you did, your beliefs,
And so much more that you planned to do and say.
All the congregations and demonstrations headed
By you, all eyes on you, for your next word, prayer,
Song and lift of everybody up and into a new day,
Some place where words take you, where dread
Cannot enter, nor what I bring to put an end
To all your good, always it is me they send.

If self could be a case filled with powder, stifled
In steel, fired in a barrel, one word in my brain,
Kill, that was me who stared into the sight on his rifle,
Latched onto you, thought no more about your life
That Memphis morning in January at the Lorraine,
Your followers in the courtyard, you on a balcony.
I am hate. I have it stenciled in my manufacture.
I dream of being the last thing to sow acrimony,

Stop love, yet here I am again in another testimony,
Of souls gathered worldwide to mark your departure,
No gladness, no air without duress, but your funeral
March to add to a life of marches, sermons, gone viral.

Forgive me, Martin. They sent me to start another war.
I do not age. I can only add to my hurts. I fight to keep
Grief as my condition, as if a Hummingbird tasted raw
Air brimming nectar, rather than the neck of flowers.
I remain the children in your big Washington speech,
Your dream stickles midstride, wings all wave and dart,
Black and white occupy space not on any timetable.
Sun and moon for tides in my pulse, if I had a heart
Like yours, so large for your chest crowds carry parts
For you, from your end through their time into table
Without end, without me, or any relative in its face,
Not as a child or flesh and blood thing but as peace.

2

Rest in me. End your journey. Let my flesh be your bed
If you promise to sleep, never rise to erase another day,
Much like the one where you searched out my voice
On your blind drive to a different place, person, time.
Did you even notice the Memphis morning sky? Red.
Breakfast talk close with friends about our next play,
Workweek, public, cherishing last night when I stood
Before a congregation, said I knew great risk follows
This path of ours that I picked without luxury of choice
In my luck, my life, if fortune helps understand mine.
Speaking for myself, I said I did not want an easy road,
Even if gardens for those routes hummed with flowers,
Fruit, longevity, and every magnetic host up above,
Meaning here on earth, all that I know, want, love.

For here I am in front of you in a white shirt, my staple.
Chest may as well be bare in my stance to receive you.
Here comes my death as I taste the morning, exhale
My worst dreams from last night: that my life thief
Shimmies up to me and catches me; that all the people
Who hear how I leave them cannot believe it to be true,
Their Martin gone, stolen from them, and such crisis

Bring some good, somehow, hard to see as heads spin,
Hands, thrown out for balance, break linked arms, fail
Legs and we fall. I say, stop, even if you burst with grief.
My abrupt end triggers some greater good. Yes, I miss
My wife, children, congregation, this world I love like sin,
Love more than myself, though love of life counts for loss
Of self, as each of us tries for one or both, win or lose.

I fall in shock but without surprise that you appear
In an instant in the middle of everything. I want it now
No other way, no second chance, nor luck. Who prays
For my last stand? I leave my warm feet, remove
Myself, float, disperse, fall back, sprinkled, into ears,
Eyes, lips, nostrils, molecular, so that all who say I won,
Or ever heard my name, everyone born in my slip stream,
Cannot help but bear me, my body reversed, returned
To molecules, digitalised, cut loose as big data. I raise
My voice. I peel my eyes wide. I take in what takes over
Me when I talk, overcome, knowing if my faith means
I pay with my last breath. I pay. All of you, stay tuned,
Your nod, hail for me, more ready for me than my words
Were for me, for this time, where even a Hummingbird

Darts too slow to slip from your sight, your sound
Laced air, left far back, target in the act of falling,
Caparisoned, always this fall, as I, me, you, us, we, drop,
Never to land, save as code made by flesh and blood,
Art, yes, but not what flesh and blood were made for,
Lacerate my body with hardly a knock, more a drive
Through me to some other place, but at a cost to me
Getting where I stand in Memphis, where Tennessee
Happens to be on the globe, and my body, soaked in
Fever before I can think, hot, muchless make sound,
Do much more than breathe out, as you divide my air
Between one Hummingbird wingbeat and the next,
Rake into my body, drill deep, and whip my soul away,
Make my words and me, at thirty-nine, last and last.

# ELIZABETH ALEXANDER

## Praise Song for the Day

*A Poem for Barack Obama's Presidential Inauguration*

Each day we go about our business,
walking past each other, catching each other's
eyes or not, about to speak or speaking.

All about us is noise. All about us is
noise and bramble, thorn and din, each
one of our ancestors on our tongues.

Someone is stitching up a hem, darning
a hole in a uniform, patching a tire,
repairing the things in need of repair.

Someone is trying to make music somewhere,
with a pair of wooden spoons on an oil drum,
with cello, boom box, harmonica, voice.

A woman and her son wait for the bus.
A farmer considers the changing sky.
A teacher says, Take out your pencils. Begin.

We encounter each other in words, words
spiny or smooth, whispered or declaimed,
words to consider, reconsider.

We cross dirt roads and highways that mark
the will of some one and then others, who said
I need to see what's on the other side.

I know there's something better down the road.
We need to find a place where we are safe.
We walk into that which we cannot yet see.

Say it plain: that many have died for this day.
Sing the names of the dead who brought us here,
who laid the train tracks, raised the bridges,

picked the cotton and the lettuce, built
brick by brick the glittering edifices
they would then keep clean and work inside of.

Praise song for struggle, praise song for the day.
Praise song for every hand-lettered sign,
the figuring-it-out at kitchen tables.

Some live by love thy neighbor as thyself,
others by first do no harm or take no more
than you need. What if the mightiest word is love?

Love beyond marital, filial, national,
love that casts a widening pool of light,
love with no need to pre-empt grievance.

In today's sharp sparkle, this winter air,
any thing can be made, any sentence begun.
On the brink, on the brim, on the cusp,

praise song for walking forward in that light.

# KWAME DAWES

## A Poem for Tuhn Das

He wakes to the crowding of birds,
he does not know their names, he has
never looked to see their colors;
as if to see them gathered by his window
would be to let them invade – they know
he is inside, they are waiting each dawn,
for him to look. He listens, a cup of coffee
in his hands, until, like a mob dispersing
the noises begin to fade, and then one
protestor remains – a cry of alarm.
His hosts ask him if he likes the sound
of the birds. They imagine that these
gentle mornings in another country,
where the air is cool early, and the sound
of neighbors slipping through the narrow
lanes, carrying only ordinary cares,
what bills to pay, what the father's
hospice care will cost, where to drink
tonight, are a healing for him, and there
in the city, birds, crowds of them
spinning in the cooler air, would seem
so alien, they will be a comfort.
He says he hears the birds – they are
startling – it is the word he uses
with the hope that they will not see
his alarm. He will never tell them
they are haunting him, following him
across the seas, over the land, waiting
to circle him and devour him – that is
his nightmare. The poet lives in exile,
this is his identity. But this is not who
he is. He is the tamer of trees,
the one who has learned an alien skill,
how to tame a boisterous tree, with pruning
and care, into something like a toy, a breathing

99

creature, small as a man's arm, the compaction
of detail, every leaf counted, every tiny
stunted limb a sinewy thing, and against
the scrim of canvas over his window,
the tree is a brief, pithy soliloquy,
like that wizened actor shuffling across
the stage, then standing in the twilight
pooling about him and saying to the world:
'They chased me deep into the night,
I changed my houses each night, and I grew
silent, keeping every dream I have had,
and every vision given to me, deep inside
me, so that they will not hear me, those
wild birds, who will follow me as far
as a man can go. Now, I am old, and dying,
and so I will step out into the light
and speak to you, tell you how to be kind
to each other, and this small secret,
that even freedom is its own prison.'
You might think that to say that this
is a dream would be to defang it of its
terror, or turn into a manageable
surrealism, but for the poet, his dreams
are the deepest truths, he wakes up
with the voice of his friends crying,
while their killers grunt with each
blunt blow of the knives, the whisper
of blood, the terrible sound of a man
saying, 'Mama, Mama, they are killing me.'


## Black Humor

*November 3, 2016*


I am, these days, mapping out the road ahead,
the way I plan a drive at dusk, choosing in my
head the paths I know best, where the lights
are always lit, and the eyelets in the streets
sparkle as guides for me. There will always

be terrors, but I have discovered a small joy
in driving alone – what I do not see, what I almost
destroy but avoid through the grace of angels,
cannot frighten blissful me. Instead, I am a ship
on a dark ocean, imagining only the universe
of monsters just beneath my hull, and the sweet
deep sleep of darkness comforts me. Of course,
it is easy to tell, perhaps, that these are the days
before the news arrives of who will lead
this country; at least so it seems, but the news
I am waiting for is the millions who will wake the day
after the count, filled with the righteous
satisfaction of having seen a restoration
of the proper order of things. It is they
I fear most, and am wary of. You see, I, too,
have walked through these eight years
as if walking inside of a miracle that has
its clear expiration date – we have done
nothing to deserve this, and soon it too,
like all products of faith, will be taken away,
so that what is left is the profit of it all,
the capacity to believe in impossible things.
This is black humor – it will be a relief
if Trump wins, it will be the end of all
passive anger, it will be the end of all
pent up resentments, it will be time again
for the sufferah to bear his sufferation
proudly with a well-trained screwface;
it will strip away the delusion of our
post-human mythos; when you shoot us
we will bleed. This is black humor:
no more dancing around the cry against
the man, the powers that be – how easy
a clean and bloody struggle is on the brain.
I am making a joke, of course, but I
must laugh in the face of what I fear:
when scowling bullies and liars win,
gloat, turn away from even the most
substantial complaint because they can,
I can either make black jokes of it all,
or I can squat in the corner and seethe.

I choose jokes. Next week, I will walk
without the soft language of a Ferrante's novels
in my head, and I will listen to the birds,
as a kind of prayer, the way prayers
attach themselves to one another,
a chain link that takes us as far back
as our long history of bewilderment
at the cycles of the universe we see takes
us – the beginning of things, always
at the beginning of things, and this too
will be yet another lovely black joke.


## Bones in the Soil


These empty landscapes; the entanglement
of trees, the river valley, the music of light
through mist; the silence – it is why I can't
make art; why I can't sit still in the dark
cave of a forest and think of anything
but spirts; well not even that but the bodies
of black people, so ordinary, so squalid,
so easilynbroken; the limbs, the ugliness
and indignity of nakedness, the disposable;
the dead end of abuse; they died here,
their flesh becoming the offence
of a stench, and then, soon, the earth
took them, and today a white man
can walk his family's acres, with easel
and canvas and brush and think: Silence,
the communion of trees, the confluence of rivers,
the chapel of light, the synod of forgetfulness.
I wish I could write myself out of such distractions.
Perhaps that is what Zen offers; you clear
your head, let oxygen enter your bones; and soon
you will see the amber of fall as only that:
leaves turning. But me, I think bones,
I think bones restless in the dark soil.

*Enoree, South Carolina*

# CLAUDIA RANKINE

## The Health of Us

We heard health care and we thought public option
we thought reaching across the street across the lines
across the aisle was the manifestation of not a red state
not a blue state but these united states we thought
we could be sure of ourselves in this one way sure
of our human element our basic decency
and if *justice was how love showed itself in public* then love
was defined by access to care when someone anyone
thought that cough that burned the chest
was probably nothing but who knew that fever
after three days that inability to breathe to sleep
to wake in justice in love we thought
we were ready to be just as good to be better
and despite all the ways we exist alone no one
would be on their own we were ready to take a stab
at a kind of human kind of union we were ready to check-up
to look after in this one way we were ready
to care for each other we were ready to see
our range of possibilities as a precious commodity
to know every other as another to live in the width
of our being and we weren't ignorant or stupid or naïve
or idealists or socialists or communists or Canadians
we understood the private options would still keep us
alive longer we understood the private options
would treat the disease not the symptoms
the private options meant access to specialists
to privacy to elective procedures to a team of doctors
to radiology imaging to brand-name drugs we understood
the impossibility of real equality but this single shift
toward a national community we thought
despite being founded on genocide and sustained by slavery
in God's country we thought we were ready
to see sanity inside the humanity we thought
the improbability of the face on capitol hill meant possibility.

# TYEHIMBA JESS

## Against Silence

• My name is Tyehimba Jess. I am a black poet. I have a silence to be rightened. I have a silence after each shooting. I remain a nation unsilenced. I am a poet murdering silence. My name is Eric. My name is Bell. My name is Eleanor. My name is nation. My rights fit any murder description. My remains remained on the asphalt for four hours while the crowd screamed about my rights. Then, the silence as I was shoved into an SUV and carted to the morgue. My name is poetic: *Trayvon, Diallo, Ousmane*, sing my blackness in the headlines. My name once held all possibilities, but now flies out from the mouth hauling anger and sorrow. I have a right to be angry. I have a morgue inside my silence. I have an arm against my throat and a bullet in my head. I have a wedding to go to, a graduation to walk, a little brother to chill with, and now I'm a face on a placard in a sea of anger, a newspaper article, I'm a question passed from one generation to the next, a lesson in fear, and all I really want is to go home. My name is murdered. My name is a silent snapshot on the funeral program. The officer remained silent. He was programmed by a nation's anger, a moaning silence born in the chokehold of a slaveship. Ask if he is a drone cruising the streets of the nation, programmed to murder black. Ask a drone for the poetry of the names of the rightless it has murdered. Ask the silence about your rights. My name is Pearly Golden. My name is Tariq Aziz. My name is Kayla Moore. My name is Aiyanna Stanley Jones. My name is Fazal Wahad. My name is a nation of funerals. The silence after my name is murdered by the sound of the next. My name is Michael Brown. My name is Kimani Gray. Kendric McDade. Mashooq Jan. Mohammad Yaas Khann. The angry drone spotted me while I was coming home from the store, on the way to work, on the way to a wedding, walking down the street. The drone looked down at me from its great height and power and the sky was full of its murder. My murder is a right this nation angers for. My name is a poem. My name is not silence. I am a black poem written into the silence left behind.

*Mashooq Jan, Fazal Wahad, Mohammad Yaas Khann, and Tariq Aziz are children murdered by U.S. drone strikes in Yemen and Pakistan. All others were murdered by U.S. police officers.*

# Habeas Corpus

*Chelsea Manning, Namir Noor-Eldeen*


You have the body, ankle and hip, each parted lip and each hair, the body with its sweatstained heat and its cough, the spleen and tongue of the body is yours from navel to spine. You have the body bundled like a fist, shuddered in darkness, bound, bloodied, under suspicion. You have the body blistered with accusation: hooded, blinded, manacled, maced. You have the body electrified, born unto the body of the republic we stand in stress position. You have the body numbered, targeted, locked, firing sequence initiated, search warrant expired when you have the body expired, exploded, the body preening in the wedding party, in a car speeding through night, in the morning before prayer, trial held in the head of the soldier flying bodiless remote drone from his body. I am the body in this voice in my silence the body rots the body unwilling to answer when you have the body and the blood on the body you have. The body stretched and waterlogged, named and unnamed, foreign and domestic, accusation in the eye of the body plucked out you have the body shipped into concrete and photographed stripped. You have the skull and the penis and the heart of the body, each vulva and opening, the digital record of the body as it writhes. You have the body definitively indefinitely, the body huddled in the shape of our body, the body you have is the body you have. You have the body.

## SHAZEA QURAISHI

## Fallujah, Basrah
*A poem in four voices*

### *Rahim*

Oh my son

Let my love
cushion the weight of your head.

Let me take your hurt
   I will hold it

while you rest
I will fold it into my body.

Sleep, my angel,
my flower, my brave, sweet boy.

> [*Child with extreme hydrocephalus – deformity of face, body
> and ear – and defects of cerebral nerves.*]

### *Sabir*

I dressed him in a long white shirt
with a blue bird embroidered over the heart
and placed tiny white mittens on his hands.
Born with thick black hair
like his father, he was almost
so beautiful, almost perfect
as we had imagined him.

> [*Born without eyes*]

*Farrah*

Where is my baby girl,
the one I dreamed?
I long for sleep
to return her.

> [*Extreme hydrocephalus. The line running down the right
> side of the head would appear to show that potentially two
> heads were forming.*]

*Anah*

> [*It isn't clear what has happened to this child.*]

NOTE: Medical quotes are taken from a report by Ross B Mirkarimi for The Arms Control Research Centre, commenting on photographs of extreme birth deformities experienced in Iraq and Afghanistan following US bombing with DU ammunition.

DALJIT NAGRA

## The Dream of Mr Bulram's English

### I

From chalk face to the latest newfangled screen
I remain an English teacher before my shades-
of-the-globe teenagers. With a click I summon
imperishable lines from our island and from abroad
for their marriage between sense and mellifluous
sentence, for the way they've jazzed our lexicon.
My awesome role's to grade but also to inspire
each teen with a lust for our courtly vowels.

### II

I pray they'll honour this tongue William dared
never to conquer, for who dare battle against
an autochthonous force. I hope to spin their minds
timeless with Chaucer, Donne, Keats and Byron,
with Tennyson and Browning. And lead them across
the spellbound shores of our tongue Shakespearean
rousing oration into stately cadence till it one day
fight on the beaches in that tongue Churchillian.

### III

If some students in the double lessons feel trapped,
if this tongue feels a curse, this flesh feels too solid
without, if this language feels ill-begot so its terms
cause shame. If we're still at sea with the whip-hand's
lashing tongue, if we're still at sea and the margin's
fading...How can we thrive in the West unless we hear,
for better or worse, the link with our distant ancestors?
This heartfelt Word, evermore, this shared tongue.

### IV

Our ancestors took on the grand dreams of the King
James Bible and grafted the English canon. I respect
the hurt but we're now in the main, now that thought

in this tongue springs universal. I wish my students peace
in a word so dignity reign. I wish them Martin Luther
King's imposing marble mimicry and free speech
steering its own course through the ruling demesne
to imply this lingua franca has become our lineage.

V

Why live in a tongue you'd hurt — you'd mercenary
grab the rules to bend, as if the migrant past justified
an off-shore narrative of high-tech fast-talk portfolios...
If my class tread on water and arrive at the isthmus
of poetry they'll find they're enshrined in high art,
they've a stake worth the investment. So I bless them
the passion of Wordsworth who saved and saved
simply to behold a canvas-bound *Arabian Nights*.

## BRIAN TURNER

## Horses

At 17 hands, their high-traction shoes clatter on the asphalt
as they canter forward, snorting, Perspex face shields a clear armor
for their wild-eyed vision of Molotov cocktails, stones, hurled debris,
the adrenaline of the boulevard ringing in the horns of their ears,
reflective shin guards glinting above mid-cannon and coronet, blare
of flashbulbs cracking the night open in a pure shock of light,
illuminating the signature of blaze and star on forehead and nose
as polycarbonate batons sing past their stiffened ears before they wheel
and turn, the boot heels of officers digging in, spurring their flanks,
the curtains of their lips pulled back by a cinching of the reins
at the bit, slobber straps wet and shining, their wide flat teeth
biting at the invisible before them as their nostrils fill with the fear
and smell of burnt exhaust, with the human calculations of misery
and pain, trajectory and loss, brokenness, ruination, the factory
of tears in its awful manufacture gone unbridled in civilisation's
rough shell, and still the officers urge *forward* as the missiles
trace a bright geometry, patient within the night's
dark fabric, the obscene beauty of it lost on no one,
as the clarity of hooves hammers against the building facades
and rises to the upper stories, just as hooves have done for millennia,
clanging through Damascus and Prague, Vladivostok and Rome,
with hussars and Cossacks and mamluks, lancers and dragoons
forming up horses abreast, the psychology of muscle and height
joined by the long history of the cavalry in its relentless charge –
the defeat of Crassus at the hands of scale-armored Parthian cataphracts
at the Battle of Carrhae, in 53 BCE; Napoleon's cuirassiers riding
headlong into the Highland squares at Waterloo; Shingen's cavalry
overrunning arquebusiers on the snowy plains of Mikata in 1573 –
and just as horses did in the days of old, these horses shove and shoulder
through the protestors in their human chicane, the trampled left
curled on the roadbed behind, wailing, as police lights strobe
the moment in a wash of red, color standard for the God of War,
the god of helmets and boots and stirrups and sweat-soaked horse blankets,
who promises steamed oats and top cut alfalfa at the road's end,
god of the threshing hooves, the riot god, who quickens panic in the driven horse

by application of the baton to the curvature of the world in its bony skull,
the god who stirs their blood into action against the refutations of consent,
pressing them on, on into the valley of placard and protest, effigies
rising from the crowd as if their leaders had lost their footing in the world
and simply rose up in flame, up to the howling god, who calls on the horses
to do the same, exhorting each to ignore the monocular field within its crazed eye,
to view the crowd from those rare heights where flame burns free of its fuel,
to rise up on its hindquarters, as in a great statue of terror, its majesty irrefutable,
the god of the loudspeaker commanding them to spark pavement and stone,
saying – *Bring your hooves down hard, my horses, bring them down.*


# Neda


Shot, her body on the street, sunlight
burns over Tehran, over the equator, the far oceans.

Tuesday afternoons. Saturday mornings.
We pass her on the bus we take to work.

We pass her on the way to the post office,
the pharmacy, the grocery store.

In Tokyo, in Rome, in Paris, the same.
She dies on these streets as she dies

in my home town of Fresno, California,
where it is early autumn and the exhausted traffic

works its way around her body on Divisidero Street,
newspapers fluttering like abandoned flags

on the pavement, like worn-out sorrows.

                    *

I wonder if someone will walk out
late one night, perhaps, to simply kneel

beside her, take her cold hand
in hand, and begin to care for her.

# The Buddhas of Bamyan

The destruction work is not as easy as people would think.

QUDRATULLAH JAMAL, Taliban Information Minister

After the shelling of artillery, with their long graceful telemetries
of explosives in flight – our stuccoed faces

crumbled and sheared free from the stone, but we did not bow down;
we stood with our backs to the sandstone cliffs, just as we did

in 1729, when Nader Shah – *the Napoleon of Persia, the Second Alexander* –
fired cannons to bring the people to their knees. These new soldiers,

do they know the old saying: *if you find the Buddha along the path,*
*strike him down*. I am Vairocana, the one of many colors.

The red one beside me, my old friend Sakyamuni. Soldiers
pay out double ropes in descent, on rappel from the crowns of our heads

with dynamite in their satchels. Such strange gifts they bring,
their faces sweating with exertion, lips chapped by thirst.

Do they know that within us the stone bleeds vermillion,
sulfides of mercury, carbonates of lead. Within us

still more Buddhas sitting cross-legged, their robes in cinnabar,
aquamarine, the creatures of dream gazing at the water's edge.

The men hanging from these braided ropes – they place their charges
in the sockets of our eyes. They lodge them in the drums

of our ears. And though our lips have crumbled to the earth
below us, our mouths are now open to the wind.

# KHALED MATTAWA

## Anthropocene Hymns

### 1

The need for armaments
as the world is reconceived
in words floating above the waters.

Thinking, planning, a dream to another,
a fellow tribesman surveying the field for a hunt,
surveying the grasslands for grazing,

a place to sleep among the trees.
The air smells of pig shit, geysers shooting
their spray, creating miniature rainbows.

### 2

The down of our nests, concrete and plastic.
The project almost completed,
taken over 2 million acres of desert lands.

Thousands of apartment blocks
awaiting further procreation.
The body politic churn must live without water now.

### 3

Churn according to theories of social change.
Yes, but for more chains, like the body's internal.
And flight? Yes, but in a tunnel, inside the churn.

### 4

What is the difference between wolf, for example,
and fox in the homeland?
Is it possible for a bird to be two birds, or four lizards?

Some rise at daybreak, others hunt at night.
Every day the same cycle, but not a churn in the absolute.
This would come later, that and the idea of value.

A churn at the level of wolves and foxes,
birds and lizards, an evolution
of traps and arrows, hides and scalping.

5

What is this clearing?
A flatness that is no longer a field,
a burning plate exhaling its final dust.

6

Is there a copulation between these two verbs,
'learn' and 'adapt',
between two concrete towers collapsing?

What are their meanings
other than
clear and burn?

7

The seasons are at work on everything,
even on themselves, an extinction here, an extension there,
some sort of algae blocking the stream, suffocating the fish –

the insects whose excrement
is turning the Taj Mahal green –
to become something, just the thing,

a new body, a new organic machine
that separates flight from body
and reserves the motions in pixels for reuse.

Gradual death as stalemate.
A détente between tumor and cell.
Live and let live.

8

To be alive then, with meaning, in a far corner,
from one's thoughts and beliefs,
to be non-human, non bird –

we have not gotten there yet.
How to stop thinking of all others as bodies,
worth extinction, worth eating or enslaving?

Once a body, it must be brought to whip or firing squad.
That's it.
The hovel, the burrow, the hive grown thin –

concrete with bones and hair mixed in.
A history enfolding, words nourished on blood.
Don't tell me we are not who we are.

### 9

You recall a certain hope
as something small, something that can fit
into a postcard of your home town.

In the long exposure image
the boulevard is streaked with car lights
red going one way, white going the other.

An image of the past that said
you had a future in the big world.
Its taste is still in your mouth after all.

### 10

The theatre inside the churn,
inside the big human cave, the chains
await the viewer like airplane seatbelts.

A faint smell of pig shit wafts through the vents.
No place else to go but this earth.
No else.

## Charlie Rose Has Frank Langella on for the Hour

Why am I here on Earth, Lord? The more these two talk, the less
of the world appears, as if they're holding a big eraser, or scrapers
or big cans of white paint spraying it all over the universe.

Langella's nose is talking about being naked in front
of the mirror – see what I mean about the world being erased? –
and he's without his Oscar nomination and without his Emmys;

and he's without his fame, and without his youth, and he's on
so many pills now – and he's got me focused on him, Lord,
on his nothingness, and Charlie Rose's. Oh, Charlie,

he's the eternal second fiddle, if ever you made one,
the eternal cheerleader, the grin, the grin that tells you, 'Do it,
go ahead, I'm with you,' whether it's bombing another country,

or sending millions to their deaths,
or using depleted uranium missiles or burning,
burning, burning the world's resources,

or any anything that smells of power and American exceptionalism,
Charlie Rose is there to support you, Lord,
and he's here nodding at Frank Langella

dabbing more white paint on the world, leaving no spot left behind
and Langella is about to weep, Lord, to weep for himself –
tears of joy about to gush from him, joy, because without his Oscar nomination,

without his Emmys, and with his white hair
and all those pills he has to take now, someone, just one person,
loves Frank Langella!

And I'm about to say Hallejluia, and Charlie Rose is grinning hallejluia,
his teeth diamonds reflecting the light of a mysterious inner life,
a light so bright it sends Langella skyward spiraling and swirling

until he forms a constellation, until he becomes a black hole
sucking up its own greatness, a giant jelly fish in the universe
taking joy from one end and producing glory from the other,

which, as you know Lord, is the pinnacle of human spirituality,
the moment when one's soul achieves the oblivion of peace
and reaches out toward the souls of late nights viewers

causing them to identify with him despite their better judgment.
I'm feeling the pull now, Lord, feeling the impossibility of my own virtue;
and my shortcomings, the aching joints of my soul, all of them are rising away

from my body, freeing me from the necessity of my own being,
announcing the inevitability of your arrival. I imagine
your surveillance cameras turned toward me at last, dear Lord,

your choppers slicing the air above me, your flashlight
aimed at my face, your bull horn calling my name,
settling me into the homeland, into the very bosom of this nation.

MARK McMORRIS

## Letter for K & Poems for Someone Else

*(a poem)*

The mirror says: a chalk house. The mirror says: leather box;
a courtyard with moss. The air frantic with fire and books
so pages fall to the cistern. The mirror's back has no silver.
The book needs to begin, needs a rose, I said, a place to sit
and study the tea that falls from the tea plant, the light
falls steady in the book, the leaves of light and of tea
in the mirror that is a book and a girl that reads looks up
a name in the moss, a green name in a red house, looks up
at *hawk*, at hawk-writing, and sees a girl in a red window
a green finger to her lips. I know her from the photo-
pictorial in the leather box. But the hawk and his name
the girl and the book; so the leaf and silver cloud, so back
and beguile; so sweater with moth-holes and scripts
from the Caliphate of WAS: they went into the book
that went into the flames. The girl and her ashes and hawk
are on a path to the courtyard; say then that the book
was banned and the tea was tea-ish, the mirror a glass.
What girl could read such a fire, what leaf would light
begin to write upon blue, or on moss, at stroke of noon?

[Letters to Michael: Dear Michael (1)]


Dear K

Found the passage you asked for
it's lovely I know you think
better of me that I like it too
that's a joke my sweet the war
bruises everyone until and even Nicole
is afraid of the government and
I miss you it's crazy to talk
this way but it must be the time.

> dis poem shall say nothing new
> dis poem shall speak of time
>
> MUTABARUKA

The larks punctuate the morning with their signals
to each other that I overhear and cannot decode
draw me from the doorway to the street, to be one
among several musics that score the city I love.
Today the Lord dies again; a scholar writes in Greek
his story of mystery; the translator comes to Antioch
to start on the final book, the one that was lost for good.
I breathe the same air and sound of voices falling
onto a page that cannot record the thing itself
how your face is close to my thought, as close as a breath
that I still listen to, a translator who keeps very still.
In one or another folio on the shelf, it says that I look
at train schedules and take steps to book your flight
dressed up for a meeting at a café. It is a volume
I want to read at once, to conclude, and start over,
a book that meets a scholar, a scholar that meets a train,
a train that meets a woman, a woman who meets me.
But this poem is like a war that never ends, this poem
has no closure, it unravels as I write, it starts again
on the Pontus Euxine, on an island, and then it says:


*(a poem)*


And so the vehicles came from driveways in the suburbs
on television the Budweiser cart brought kegs to a tavern
a game was decided in the final seconds, and the war –
the war was pictures and absence, and folks ran up the flags
over the middle country, the coasts and the South, bewildered
and yet relieved to see all that power, that certainty of might.
Some said that night would never end, had been a war
since 1453     or 1097    /    or 410      or 336 BC
had been continuous combat since Helen gave Paris a flower
at least since the Bronze Age of Agamemnon's armada.

I had no time for the war. The bundle asleep on a ventilator
was a person under folds of thin cloth; I had no time
for this individual who was as good as dead, in this city
of memorials to the dead. The seat of a new *imperium*,
the White House said freedom and meant that the dead
are free to trouble each other. I had no time for the dead.


.   .   .   .


Since the Hittites rode on chariots, and there was script.

In caustic time, since Byblos fell to Alexander, since Damascus
to the English lion; and since Hektor, tamer of horses
and since Dunkirk and Bosnia fell to enemy phalanxes.

In caustic time, since Balaclava, Barcelona
since Byron fell asleep on the Aegean, and since Kuwait
fell to the tanks and Agincourt to the bowmen and since
Baghdad fell to Crawford in Texas, and Archimedes
built his engines and fell to a legionnaire – I am perfectly
sane – and since Delhi fell to the Indians, as was right,
and since the Orange Street holocaust in Kingston.

And in that time, since a scholar read old Egyptian
and brought an obelisk to the Place de la Concorde
(the circle of harmony), and since the Tutsis or the Kikuyu
or since the Xhosa or the Taino, I have no time for this.
The year is not yet ripe

                                        to read novels as the bombs fall
to study the *Phaedrus* or go bowling and have a pancake
or to be ordinary and to fix a broken door lock. I disagree.
It is better to shine shoes than to starve, I can't agree.
I know nothing about it. It is better to pick apples – or slash cane –
on earth than to lie under it. I have no time for questions.
Bring the troops home, people do Vandal, they riot in America
I see it on television. Cherry blossoms are falling there love.

I remember the blossoms. The light falls like blossoms.

Everything falls, to pieces, to the victor, to someone's lot
falls like a girl falls or a blossom, falls head over heels
like a city or water and like darkness falls, a dynast
a government can fall, or an apple, a cadence, the side of a hill.
The road can fall to the sea, the land in the ascent, o sky.
Doom like a knife in the chest, this falls
and has fallen from spear points and rifles, blades of light
that cut through the skin of a lemon and peel away doubt
falls into line with opinion I know what you think
a glance can fall like doom and therefore like a knife and a river
this makes no sense I have no time for metaphor or you or this
falls or I will more than my share and you will have less
oh yes, the water can fall like a sky and a lot
like a blossom in the dusk, and a scepter falls to the mat
the Fall of Byzantium was not so long ago that it falls
out of mind like a person from a moving streetcar, always
I said that the light falls on lilacs in the window box
the features on a coin fall away and the era of mosques, this
time of cathedrals and temples, and the long fall of Lucifer
to his kingdom on earth and our falling is always falling.


*(a poem)*

When the combat finally stops, then I will come to you
like a soldier to his commander, and you will decorate my chest
with fingers too soft and too precious for other uses, asking
my kill rate and praising my accurate eye, the night of lemon
blossoms perfuming your under arms, your heart's land
undressed for my touch and my guilt abolished, the blood
left on the porch. The cicadas will trumpet my coming
and cancel the shriek of Tomahawks and soothe my ears.

When the combat ceases for good, I will put off the clothes
stained with shit and gunpowder, the boots eaten away
and my rusty helmet, and dress up to suit your dignity.
I will have cherry blossoms or the photo of a yellow poui
and they will speak on my behalf of the continuous war
the war that is falling in and out of the signal's compass
the signal I rode on to this gate that creaks behind me.
Combat spells the end of civility but I must begin with you.

When the combat ends, and bulldozers have crushed the shanties
and ploughed a thousand or five corpses under the pasture
the young man has lost his legs, and has questions for someone
and the vehicles head home to Greenwich and the janitors
empty the trash, and the captains hold their fire. At that time
but at no time does the war cease from thunder and the crack
of a rifle, and the book of your labyrinth has no beginning
or foreseeable respite, and I must retreat as I approach.

When the combat closes down, look for me in Tempe
and you should expect some ceremony in my face
because when the war goes bankrupt and is swallowed up
then it will be time to drink a toast, and to get on with it,
one on one, one kiss or word at a time, in good time.

*16 April 2003*

## Untitled

The state created the wall
Dividing the body of the city
The separate parts do not touch
The peril of the wall slices
Through the city like a machete

In the ghetto made by the wall
The ordeal is not avoidable
You must go through the labyrinth
Your mouth full of anguish
The arrival of the wall over and over

Like standing in one place
The same liquor store
The same shuttered warehouse
The same dollar store
Like walking the same block
The same elevated track
Bordering the schoolyard

The wall goes through your vision
The wall is a projected face
Across the bedrooms of the city
Attracting the weather, the sky leaking
Nails on the surroundings

A barrier, the wall is flat
A screen, the wall is a surface
Like a page or a window
In negative space
The wall is grim language
Showing things outside

Faces visible under lines
Of drawing, marked by fear

The separate parts of the city

The wall projects repeatedly
The same dollar store

The same elevated track
Over schoolyards

HONORÉE FANONNE JEFFERS

## Blues for Harpsichord, or, the Boston Massacre

*The death of Crispus Attucks, Boston, March 5, 1770*

Blamed, charged, scattered kin, auctioned memories –
        this for black men, but for their masters? Toys.

Music of the rich, a myth in near-spring,
        tame, wet times of those rich, bewigged white boys.

Wives rendered blind – necessary – sway
        in their tight panniers, waists bone-threaded.

(Taken care of.) In this calm scene, there's lace –
        outside – reality – slippery steps

to walk, and then: stinking wharfs, those big ships
        disgorging tea, African, sad stuffing.

Redcoats shoot Crispus-the-Brave on streets slick
        with outrage and brethren's gore, snow muffling

truth, deaf to the harpsichord's free, blued daze.
        Black prelude. Black fugue. Black glittered affray.


## Mothering #2

*Someplace in Senegambia Region, c. 1761*

> 'Twas mercy brought me from my Pagan land,
> Taught my benighted soul to understand...
> PHILLIS WHEATLEY


*Mercy, child.*
What a mother might have said, pointing

at the sun rising, what makes life possible.
Then dripped the bowl of water,

reverent, into oblivious earth.
Was this prayer for her?

Respect for the dead or disappeared?
An act to please a genius child?

Her little girl could speak
only of water, bowl, sun –

light arriving,
light gone –

sometime after the nice white lady
paid and named her for the slave ship.

*Mercy*: what the child called Phillis
claimed after that sea journey.

Journey.
Let's call it that.

Let's lie to each other.

Not early descent into madness.
Naked travail among filth and rats.

What got Phillis over the sea?
What kept a stolen daughter?

Perhaps it was *mercy*,
Dear Reader.

*Mercy*,
Dear Brethren.

Water, bowl, sun –
a mothering, God's milky sound.

Morning shards, and she wondered
if her child forgot her real name,

refused to envision the rest:
baby teeth missing

and somebody wrapping her treasure
(barely) in a dirty carpet.

*'Twas mercy.*
You know the story –

how we've lied to each other.

# ARUNDHATHI SUBRAMANIAM

## Prayer

May things stay the way they are
in the simplest place you know.

May the shuttered windows
keep the air as cool as bottled jasmine.
May you never forget to listen
to the crumpled whisper of sheets
that mould themselves to your sleeping form.
May the pillows always be silvered
with cat-down and the muted percussion
of a lover's breath.
May the murmur of the wall clock
continue to decree that your providence
run ten minutes slow

May nothing be disturbed
in the simplest place you know
for it is here in the foetal hush
that blueprints dissolve
and poems begin,
and faith spreads like the hum of crickets,
faith in a time
when maps shall fade,
nostalgia cease
and the vigil end.

## Madras, November, 1995

Secret garden, swimming
in the amniotic light of a green afternoon,
where the trees are familiar, the pink musanda,
the thunder's north-eastern baritone and its subtexts,
where much lies buried beneath generations of soil
and the thick sugarcane slush of rain –

a cosmic despair over algebra homework
rising with the aroma of turmeric and damp jasmine,

the silent horror of my grandmother
who watched her husband drive away her cats
through the stern geometry of her kitchen window,

my fourteen-year-old indignations
near dusty bougainvillea tresses
at belonging to a tribe of burnished brahmins
that still likes to believe its skin is curdled vanilla,

and the long amorous wail
of confectioned Tamil film songs
from the transistor of a neighbour's gardener, long dead.

No, I am not sentimental
about the erasure of dynastic memories,
the collapse of ancestral houses,
but it will be difficult to forget
palm leaves in the winter storm,
ribbed, fossilised,
against heaving November skies,
building up their annual heritage of anguish
before the monsoons end.

# GREGORY PARDLO

## Winter After the Strike

Perhaps we are each a cresting echo hesitating, vibrant with the moment
before rippling back.

But you're steadfast as one strapped to the mast, as you were
in '81 when Reagan ordered you back to work. You were president

of the union local you steered with your workingman's voice,
the voice that ground the Ptolemaic ballet of air traffic to a temporary stop.

You used it to refuse to cross the picket line I walked
with you outside Newark International.

I could see the dark Turnpike for miles, the somber
office buildings winking insomniac cells, the tarmac

spread before us like a picnic blanket and you, like a jade Buddha
suffused in the glow of that radial EKG.

You'd push the microphone in front of me, nod, and let me give the word.
I called all my stars home, trajectories bent on the weight of my voice.

You say you miss tracking those leviathans, each one snagged on the barb
of your liturgy. I too, get reeled in by the hard, now rusty music of your pipes.

I follow it back to the day of your accident in the story you tell:
you were sixteen, hurdling the railings dividing row house porches

from one end of Widener Place to the other to impress Mom.
I imagine the way you cleared each one like a leaf bobbing on water, catching

the penultimate, the rubber toe of your Chuck Taylors kissed
by the rail, upsetting your rhythm and you roiled in the air headlong,

arms outstretched, stumbling toward the last like one hell bent
or sick to the stomach. The way you landed, on your throat, the rail

could have taken your head clean off. Since then, your voice issues
like some wartime communiqué: a ragged, type-written dispatch

which you swallow with your smoker's cough black as a tire
spinning in the snow. That winter after the strike,

we were so poor you sold everything but the house. Tell me, Dad,
when you'd stand at the door calling me in for the night,

could you hear me speaking to snowflakes falling beneath the lamppost?
Could you hear me out there imitating you imitating prayer?

NATHALIE HANDAL

## Letter from the Levant

There is no city behind the window. No place of worship. No stars between our stories. No gleaming meadow. The ruins we never named are endless. The survivors our scars. We have to believe God is the faint resonance inside, that silence will take eternity apart and hang it on death's small door. It's true, once we knew every stop on the Palestine Railway. Now from other windows, we still see the route to Baghdad, Homs to Tripoli, Baalkek to Beirut, Tyre to Acre, Haifa to Jaffa, Jerusalem to Gaza before Alexandria. Now from distant places we read postcards that say, *my hands are for my absence only*. We pretend not to believe. Where we come from the truth never disturbs the horse in our sleep. We close our hands to forget what we know and are unable to tell.

## Noir, *une lumière*

There is a sorceress in our night. A sky that only moves memory to make place for the mangoes of last month. There is an old man who says, *Libère moi*. And means, Take everything but my blackness. Only in the dark do doves find reason. Only in the dark do doves have reason to believe that vengeance is light hanging on fallen tree. After each fall, we ask, where is the island, the sugarcane that disappeared in our hunger, the water that emptied our thirst, the song that robbed our nightmare? They mock us. They tell us to whisper in their ears. They will obey. But curses beat the air wild. The air is faint. And they tell us, *Stop plotting fire. You are in the wrong land even if the roosters recognise you*. They hated our black. What they didn't understand is that it illuminates their world.

# I Am Going to Speak About Liberty

I don't feel this closing as an islander. I'm not closed because I'm a peasant or a farmer or a passerby. I don't feel this closing because I'm Catholic, Protestant, Muslim, or atheist. I'm close to what's closed inside of me. If I weren't a poet, I'd still feel it. If I weren't born, I'd still feel it. I'm close to what's closed inside of me. My closing can be explained. It's far inside history. I chase it away, it returns. It comes from the waves from the winds from the birds that can't see obscurity or the shadows that insist on dying each day. I'm close to what's closed inside of me. I look at the mother looking at her child eating – why isn't she smiling? I look at my lover looking at me naked beside him – why isn't he smiling? I look at the ex-slave growing mangoes, and his daughters drinking water from a well – why aren't they smiling? I always believed that everything was black and white. But what's closed inside of me isn't black or white. If you put it in a dark room, it wouldn't find the brightness of arcs, and if you put it in a room of light, it wouldn't find darkness unlocking. I'm close to what's closed inside of me. Where else can I find an ode I understand.

*After César Vallejo*

# ROGER ROBINSON

## Nightshift

*(for the cleaning women of Brixton Nightshift)*

With the stars scattered in the sky
like dust In a dim light.
I'm travelling of the N109 bus
rolling over grit in the asphalt.
Is 3am and everybody sleeping
And these three Nigerian women are
all red eye tired, as one nods her head.
but they can't go to bed
'cause they going west end to clean
some rich mans building.
Whilst everybody sleep and dream
is bubbling water and mop and stretch
and wipe and soap and cloth and steam.
But here on the bus is bubbling gossip
and strong thick coffee, a smiling laughing scene.
Last shift was three hours ago so one of them head dropping low
only to be woken each time by their laughter
On the streets ravers are heading home
with smudged mascara and damp hair.
These Nigerian women
when they get to their buildings
they will unwrap their head
ties and fold away their dutch print wraps
for a pale blue apron  and a pink plastic
hair protector, a bucket, a mop and chamois cloth.
Look up in any building at night
you will see their silhouette wiping, wiping
away the dust and grime of yesterday's bankers.
Suspended in the air between heaven and earth
the choreography every night. Backs bent and stretch
and wipe backs bent stretch and wipe
suds bubbling  in steaming water
toilet after toilet after toilet an aching back,
some swollen knuckles and aching wrists.

Mopping away they own footsteps
but there are small children waiting
on small wages for Garri school shoes
and books in Lagos.
So they must dance their dance
with these hoovers in office from morning till midnight.
But for now in the dim light of this N109
they are laughing and smiling even though
rumbling stomachs lined with dry bread
and the stars are scattered in the sky
above the bus like dust in a dim light.


## Killing Suite for Stephen Lawrence


I remember that night we heard our faces became creased cracked
and creviced as earthquakes.

Expressions tightened like tension in tug o war ropes
Even the clouds in the night air were sympathetic

Rolling like milk in black tea or billowing like blood in water depending on
your point of view

We were the ones walking dead in all but name
Yawning yelping yearning voices of angered passion

with no answer but for muted thunder with a rasping edge
You the vibrant man boy your life cleaved away like fat from meat

looking forward to girlfriends graduations and good times
Listening to hip hop at the bus stop in your headphones

Its tinny drum ringing in you ear the last sound you'd hear
as you struggled to escape sleeps vivid mire

and I, I used to believe in love justice karma and hope
but I guess there ain't no love justice karma and hope

for black boys gagging in a pool of blood at the bus stop
with hip hop in their headphones

There's a darker side to this death
the side that makes a father bury his face in his hands

I heard you were buried facing the dawn
to avoid the smell of storms floating blood and evil spirits

I shall grab loose soil from your grave in my clawed fist
and point lighted candles to the sky and smile

in this service attended by myself and the wind.

Take this poem I wrote about police sealing her life with masking tape

Cursing them with the breaths she didn't know would be her last

Take this poem about whose punctured head dripped like an egg timer

filled with blood
the echo in his cell the only answer to his scream for help
what good are poems, what's their use other than to soak up spilled blood
or to wipe away tears of grieving families

Here take all these poems no ink scribbled on paper
gave them one single extra heart beat or an extra tide of breath surging
from their lungs

And until poems can bring these lives back they're worth nothing
They're worth absolutely nothing at all.

MAJOR JACKSON

## Going to Meet the Man

As if one day, a grand gesture of the brain, an expired
subscription to silence, a decision raw as a concert
of habaneros on the lips: a renewal to decency like a trash
can smashing a storefront or the shattering glass face
of a time-clock: where once a man forced to the ground,
a woman spread-eagled against a wall, where a shot into
the back of an unarmed teen: finally, a decisive spark,
the engine of action, this civilian standoff: on one side,
a barricade of shields, helmets, batons, and pepperspray:
on the other, a cocktail of fire, all that is just and good.

## Stand Your Ground

*(a double golden shovel)*

America, how often I have applauded your flag-poles. We,
as citizens, struggle to find common ground, yet do
much to damage the planks of your Ark. Not
a soft tune we make, glissando of the harmonised. We have a want
problem: more of ourselves problem, Us versus Them
in the great race to prosperity. In his Introduction to
Metaphysics, Heidegger asks 'Why are there beings at all?' We have
as guides: Klansmen and eugenicists, who proclaim all others are less.
It is, I admit, the slapping of your ropes tolling a perfect union. But,
is the measure of your worth a silent clang elsewhere? How is it
a ripple also runs through me when your wind rises? Your cloth is
nation, hauled down or half-mast, like a deferred dream only
earthly because we strive on a path hidden by dead leaves, a natural
entity whose death makes valid its rebirth, – that
an angry man can shoot a teenager is par, as we say. We,
Iota, Deltas, Crips, Knights, new tribesmen in new codes, should
in earnest put away our swords and talk-shows. Think:
our watermelons have so many seeds, and we,

136

galaxy in us, dissolve our supernovas. The mysteries we have,
an unmitigated burning of sound and fury, not
organism of one, but organs. America, I've had enough.


## On Disappearing


I have not disappeared.
The boulevard is full of my steps. The sky is
full of my thinking. An archbishop
prays for my soul, even though
we met only once, and even then, he was
busy waving at a congregation.
The ticking clocks in Vermont sway

back and forth as though sweeping
up my eyes and my tattoos and my metaphors,
and what comes up are the great paragraphs
of dust, which also carry motes
of my existence. I have not disappeared.
My wife quivers inside a kiss.
My pulse was given to her many times,

in many countries. The chunks of bread we dip
in olive oil is communion with our ancestors,
who also have not disappeared. Their delicate songs
I wear on my eyelids. Their smiles have
given me freedom which is a crater
I keep falling in. When I bite into the two halves
of an orange whose cross-section resembles my lungs,

a delta of juices burst down my chin, and like magic,
makes me appear to those who think I've
disappeared. It's too bad war makes people
disappear like chess pieces, and that prisons
turn prisoners into movie endings. When I fade
into the mountains on a forest trail,
I still have not disappeared, even though its green facade

turns my arms and legs into branches of oak.
It is then I belong to a southerly wind,
which by now you have mistaken as me nodding back
and forth like a Hasid in prayer or a mother who has just
lost her son to gunfire in Detroit. I have not disappeared.

In my children, I see my bulging face
pressing further into the mysteries.

In a library in Tucson, on a plane above
Buenos Aires, on a field where nearby burns
a controlled fire, I am held by a professor,
a General, and a photographer.
One burns a finely wrapped cigar, then sniffs
the scented pages of my books, scouring
for the bitter smell of control.
I hold him in my mind like a chalice.
I have not disappeared. I swish the amber
hue of lager on my tongue and ponder the drilling
rigs in the Gulf of Alaska and all the oil-painted plovers.

When we talk about limits, we disappear.
In Jasper, TX you can disappear on a strip of gravel.

I am a life in sacred language.
Termites toil over a grave,
and my mind is a ravine of yesterdays.
At a glance from across the room, I wear
September on my face,
which is eternal, and does not disappear
even if you close your eyes once and for all
simultaneously like two coffins.

# IV

# TERRANCE HAYES

## American Sonnet for My Past and Future Assassin

When MLK was shot, his blood changed to change
Wherever it hit the floor. Like the others, Jackson
And Abernathy gathered a few coins for themselves.
Some were the size of buttons, thin as communion
Wafers, made of gold, bronze all kinds of metals.
A maid sold the penny she found for a pretty penny on
The black market. It's in a display case beside the bullets
Dubois kept in the shotgun under his bed. Marcus
Garvey sat on a horse so tall, he disappeared.
Malcolm X grew large as the roots of an aspen
Crisscrossing the landscape. In the game of 'Chicken'
Two drivers speed at each other & if someone
Does not swerve, both drivers may die in the crash.
This country is mine as much as orphan's house is his.

# JERICHO BROWN

## Bullet Points

I will not shoot myself
In the head, and I will not shoot myself
In the back, and I will not hang myself
With a trashbag, and if I do,
I promise you, I will not do it
In a police car while handcuffed
Or in the jail cell of a town
I only know the name of
Because I have to drive through it
To get home. Yes, I may be at risk,
But I promise you, I trust the maggots
And the ants and the roaches
Who live beneath the floorboards
Of my house to do what they must
To any carcass more than I trust
An officer of the law of the land
To shut my eyes like a man
Of God might, or to cover me with a sheet
So clean my mother could have used it
To tuck me in. When I kill me, I will kill me
The same way most Americans do,
I promise you: cigarette smoke
Or a piece of meat on which I choke
Or so broke I freeze
In one of these winters we keep
Calling worst. I promise that if you hear
Of me dead anywhere near
A cop, then that cop killed me. He took
Me from us and left my body, which is,
No matter what we've been taught,
Greater than the settlement a city can
Pay a mother to stop crying, and more
Beautiful than the brand new shiny bullet
Fished from the folds of my brain.

## Second Language

You come with a little
Black string tied
Around your tongue,
Knotted to remind
Where you came from
And why you left
Behind photographs
Of people whose
Names need no
Pronouncing. How
Do you say God
Now that the night
Rises sooner? How
Dare you wake to work
Before any alarm?
I am the man asking,
The great grandson
Made so by the dead
Tenant farmers promised
A plot of land to hew.
They thought they could
Own the dirt they were
Bound to. In that part
Of the country, a knot
Is something you
Get after getting knocked
Down, and story means
Lie. In your part
Of the country, class
Means school, this room
Where we practice
Words like *rope* in our
Hope to undo your
Tongue, so you can tell
A lie or break a promise
Or grow like a story.

## Stand

Peace on this planet
Or guns glowing hot,
We lay there together
As if we were getting
Something done. It
Felt like planting
A garden or planning
A meal for a people
Who still need feeding,
All that touching or
Barely touching, not
Saying much, not adding
Anything. The cushion
Of it, the skin and
Occasional sigh, all
Seemed like work worth
Mastering. I'm sure
Somebody died while
We made love. Some-
Body killed somebody
Black. I thought then
Of holding you
As a political act. I
May as well have
Held myself. We didn't
Stand for one thought,
Didn't do a damn thing,
And though you left
Me, I'm glad we didn't.

## CAMILLE T. DUNGY

## The Preachers Eat Out

*Vernon Johns*

There were maybe four of them, perhaps five.
They were headed, where? It does not matter,
only, they were not home yet, were not near
anyone who could have cared. So hungry,
they stopped there anyway. And when they heard,
*We don't serve your kind*, one among them laughed,
*That's okay. We're not hungry for our kind.*
*We've come for food.* And when the one waitress
who would serve them – she had children at home
and these were tips – finished breaking their plates
behind the building, he called her over
to the table. *Lady, my one regret*
*is that we don't have appetite enough*
*to make you break every damned plate inside this room.*

## Greyhound to Baton Rouge

Certainly they all understood the law,
but the white lady four rows from the front
and next to the one free seat took the child
and made the tired mother, *Sit right down.*

Arm around his wife, the new father stood,
relieved to see his baby still sleeping.
Small peace.

        Sunday last he preached a story
like this. Remember Mary and Joseph
with their child? Do not forget they were chased
by the demands of one man.

                              The driver
surprised no one. *I will not move this bus,*
*you hear?* The colored bus he ordered came,
empty, just for them. *Go now. Take your wife.*
*Boy, get your baby out the lady's hands.*


## My Grandmother Takes the Youth Group to Services


The sky's wide open blue told her, *Go in*
*where you have never been before,* and where
she went she took the children. Older girls
in long skirts, little black heels, white collars
rough with starch, and hair still hot from the comb,
along with boys their age, pants creased, shoes blacked
and bright. Little Linda in Topeka
had upset no one yet, but that black shock,
Lynchburg's largest high school class in years, did.

Surprised, the white minister welcomed her
with silence, but that evening his voice fumed
through Thornton's phone. *Your pretty wife should trust*
*the good Lord's plan. Let her know, in heaven,*
*negroes will have to learn their rightful place.*


## Brevity


            As in four girls; Sunday
dresses: bone, ash, bone, ash, bone, ash, bone.

## Dear Empire,

These are your dissidents. They are dark and threadbare like the stripped corpses of trees in winter. They feather the hillsides in their cloth houses. Whole hillsides are awash in bright fabric – riverbeds of canvas.

At night, the valley is a galaxy of small fires. There are songs that can be heard above the shelling in the distance. Sometimes the thuds are percussion for their songs.

This year is growing long, and the ravines have lost their grasses. What shall we do? The winter rains will wash them out as one sweeps bits of dust to the floor. What shall we do with these bodies at the gate?

## Dear Empire,

These are your refugees. The tents they use to cover their heads are made of a soft, translucent fabric. When the winds spill from down the mountain, the tents inflate like the sails of a ship. The whole valley is adrift in an arid sea. And when the sun shines upon the tents, you can see the shadows of the people against the rippling curtains of silk:

Here is a family, the dark face of the mother is turned to one side, then disappears as the walls of the tent fold inward. And here is a child with a ball. Here is an old woman with her back pressed against the walls of cloth, craning her head as though she were listening to music from beyond the camp. As though she were filled with the expectation of water in a very hot month.

From the mountains above the camp, the tents are the egg sack of a giant amphibian, the living hearts beating clear in a clutch of embryos.

**RAE PARIS**

## To the Killers of Us

*for the friend who gifted me a phrase shared in this poem*

What did you do to us?
Did you drink our skin,
make tea from the powdered layers?

Did you weave our coffins
with hair from our own heads,
was this you?

And what of the whorls
that used to grace our fingers?
What happened to the trace of us?

Are we the ones who scream at your deathbed?
Were we the ones who said we forgive you,
who sometimes beat and call our women bitches,
tell them to fuck off and get the fuck out, who remove
our tongues to kiss men in dented corners, wake
with your name stuck in our teeth or branded on our cheek,
who tell stories of bright rooms and closed familiar hands when
we're too young, or gaping sidewalks when we're old enough
to watch you choke us again and again while we yell,
We can't –
or say nothing,
was this us?

Who were we then?
What are we becoming?

Some days we wonder what is left for us to love.
Some days we wonder what's left of us.

Tell us.

You who have taken almost everything,
but this white butterfly holding onto purple
for dear life, or the sweat that comes from
bucking bales, or seeding sweet corn we planted
with hands we trace from singing
the million ways Black and Brown hearts die
and live, still we live
stories no one believes or wants to hear,
like the love that rinses our tilted tear gassed faces
into a milky caul,
or the small passing of sage our nephew bound,
juniper, yellow and red roses,
into our open hands,
true true medicine, ours to burn
and bathe in smoke,
stoke each heart and limb
for that next time fire.
See –

You have not taken any of these things,
not the music or the beat or the drum we hollowed
from cottonwood, cut on our land, strung with animals
we soaked and dried our own selves, these skins,
the remains of our staggered breath,
yes,
we, the *survivor of many*,
who will love and live still,
we know what you've done,
we're telling who you are.

*Taos, New Mexico, 2015*

# PHILIP METRES

## Compline

That we await a blessed hope, & that we will be struck
With great fear, like a baby taken into the night, that every boot,

Every improvised explosive, Talon & Hornet, Molotov
& rubber-coated bullet, every unexploded cluster bomblet,

Every Kevlar & suicide vest & unpiloted drone raining fire
On wedding parties will be burned as fuel in the dark season.

That we will learn the awful hunger of God, the nerve-fraying
Cry of God, the curdy vomit of God, the soiled swaddle of God,

The constant wakefulness of God, alongside the sweet scalp
Of God, the contented murmur of God, the limb-twitched dream-

Reaching of God. We're dizzy in every departure, limb-lost.
We cannot sleep in the wake of God, & God will not sleep

The infant dream for long. We lift the blinds, look out into ink
For light. My God, my God, open the spine binding our sight.

## Testimony
*(after Daniel Heyman)*

I sit in a hotel room and draw this Iraqi.
The question is: how to fill the frame
With each etched face, each bound body.
*They stripped the father and son,* this man says,

████████████████████████████

*They made the father strike the son.*

Son and father    the stripped they, I write.
I listen as I draw and try to disappear
And make the father strike his son
███████████████████████

While I draw and try to disappear
Scratches turn into words, ██████.

Hovering in words around his unbound head,
Like a hovering mother or torturer
Scratches turn into words, ██████:
*They could not make son hit the father.*
███████████████████████

I sketch with a stylus on a copper plate

Father    ██hit son    make not    could they
███████████████████████
███████████████████████
How *they made the father dig a hole*
The words scratched backwards, as in a mirror.
*And they made the son get into the hole.*

How they made the father dig a hole
I have to write very quickly
How they made the son get into the hole
And *made the father bury him up to his neck.*
I have to write very quickly
So I do not lose the ██████████

And made the father bury him up to his neck
*And later ride him like a donkey.*
So I do not lose ██████████
Each etched face, each bound body
And later ride him like a donkey –
I sit in a hotel room and draw this Iraqi.

## AMALI RODRIGO

## Kolmanskop

*A ghost town*


I was sun-blind and listening to the sound of water
in wind, in desert sand, water in everything but

the river or the low trough where horses once drank
the sky. What survives is a tiny archipelago of wrecks,

the river an artery that bled out and out, became
an emboss of bone and I want to ask you if you truly

believe it is brave to enlist in war that is like the distant
sound of water with its cryptic messages of *a safer world*.

Thinking of you entering airspace, anonymous over sleep,
to leave trails of diamonds on the earth in one burst

of creation and your getaway mistaken for a star's blink,
can I forgive that you can't tell apart fleeing from stalking:

people beneath your bombs or prospectors straggling
across a desert to Kolmanskop driven by legends

of diamonds the size of men's hearts on riverbeds, as if
the milky way was laid down on earth for the picking?

From your great height you can't see how they lope alike,
mile by blistered mile, emptying of words, bearings –

some to find anyone who will save them, others not believing
they were only passing through, building houses, great halls

for opera now filling with wind's arias – men moving
too swiftly for the earth's slow kindling of diamonds.

All mined out, night in a ghost town is an armoured hood
with its shrapnel of stars. Soon you'll come, my wish,

my safe passage to a mythic lode, I too will say nothing,
taste the fine brine of your sweat, drink every cup of sand.


## The Eye


wants to be flung at everything, because it can
haul back or hoard, what's tugging to escape.

When its slow accretion like bric-à-brac
on a windowsill foreshadows the give

and take of a view, the Eye learns to high-step, turn
bird shaped. Sometimes it believes

in the eye of a Great Skua, who dives and dives
at intruders near nests, always missing the trick

of a raised hand; that the most visible part
of a thing, is not necessarily its weakest, nor all.

The Eye wants to hang back in a time
when bombs were new, pictures, uncensored

when a severed arm would not be replaced
by a bloodied shirt. Now, when smoke mushrooms

on skylines, Eyes fall to earth in great numbers, stagger
everywhere, half relieved they can't undo

what they don't have eyes to see. Sometimes
the Eye dreams of being a white elephant, rare

and auspicious, but is often fated to a vigil
on the sidewalk listening for a clink in the cup.

The Eye yokes itself to another to find depth
in the world, now and then, the calibration off-shot

as though through tears, it can't keep
from emptying all at once. The Eye is helpless

to stop the dilating iris from yielding
to remnants of light and sometimes, all it wants

is to be the gull that dips into the arched dark
beneath a bridge, and never comes out.


## Peace

*Sri Lanka, 2011*


Within weeks of war's end, women everywhere began to find teeth marks on their breasts and bellies, often on the tenderest parts of their upper arms. Some woke to it after a restful sleep. Some were roused past midnight, finding no cause, turned over a new leaf of sleep. Days passed. Each found an echo of a narrative but no memory. Each found, how this confluence grew into a naked man, slathered in black grease, all of him faintly glistening as he moved like a night-river. They named it the *Grease Devil*.

In naming, this singular pain grew worse, so did the devil's ardour and night after night blood tie-died their sheets. Village men banded for vigilante night watch. Clutching at shadows, all they ever came away with were blackened, slick palms. Often there wasn't even that. If sometimes, a woman found flecks of skin beneath her own fingernails, she thought nothing of it.

One night, when they were all out to lasso this night-river, memories found them staring downstream with arms upraised as if in praise or supplication or surrender. When they came to, no one could tell which. But they sensed peace.

I could say peace was a river with time on its hands or a white elephant escaped from memory. I could say peace was stubborn as a water buffalo or shy as a sun-basking snake noosed in grass. But it wasn't like that. Peace waited all night to take in the faithless lover. Peace cursed like a fishwife brimful of toddy with her man so much at sea. Peace was less a woman with bitten breasts, though even now, some claim otherwise.

# FADWA SULEIMAN

## *from* **Genesis**
*translated from the Arabic (Syria) by Marilyn Hacker*


Rain on rain
And mud on mud
My grandmother weaves the story
With a thread of sun
And a thread of moon
She grinds her words
In the mill of her breath, and scatters them
Among the stars

\* \*

Rain on rain
And mud on clay
My grandmother turns with the earth
And kneads sand into her wine
At moonrise

\* \*

Rain on rain
And mud on mud
She attaches the sea to a pen
And spreads its breath on a page
She dries the salt on her knees
Gives birth to clouds
She makes fountains of her breasts
Gives birth to the grass

\* \*

Rain on rain
And mud on clay
At night my grandmother sows cities
That grow at daybreak
And she sings to the reeds

\* \*

Rain on rain
He writes on the clay
We have taken the one in the sky as our witness
And he said
The sky comes from you
The sky is for you
My grandmother locked
All the doors with the cry of her blood

\* \*

Rain on rain
And the clay tablets say
We have taken the one in the sky as our witness
He asked for blood
And would not accept our harvests
My grandmother barricaded
The doors with the cry of her blood

\* \*

Rain on rain
Blood on the grass
And grass above the blood
Blood leads to blood
Half of you will be slaughtered by the other half
And the sky has locked its doors

\* \*

Rain on rain
And mud on mud
She bends her neck to the wind
And her waist to the trunk of a fruit-tree
Bends her knees to the pebbles
And her forehead to the dust
She offers her fingers to the bees
And her teeth to the truth
Her songs to the reeds
And her feet to the roots
Her blood to the wedding of seed and flower
She lets her hair down over the story

\* \*

Rain on rain
And mud on clay
My grandmother sets her fingers on fire waiting
For a prodigal to return
She gives off an odor of blood
My grandmother is still a virgin

\* \*

Rain on rain
And mud on mud
Each time a herd of gazelles goes by
They are devoured by hunters
Who already had eaten their fill

\* \*

Salt on a wound
And water on mud
We are only memories
In flight across time

# CHOMAN HARDI

## Gas Attack

*Badria Saeed Khidir and Ayshe Maghdid Mahmud*


Bombs could fall anywhere, any time of the day.
They were a nuisance we got used to. In our
dug out shelters we felt safe, until that haunting

winter twilight when the muffled explosions
deceived us. We came out thinking we'd survived
the bombs but a chalky-yellow powder settled

on our skin, smelling of sweet apples at first,
seemed safe to breathe in. People were going crazy
laughing, buckling at the knees, twisting, running

to the water source, blinded, bumping into trees.
Villagers from the region came to our aid. They said
my son looked strange, as if his eye colour had spilt

out, his face was blistered, blackened. He groaned
like a calf faced with the knife. I was still blind when he
died, could not see him, did not say goodbye.


## Dibs Camp, the Women's Prison

*Nabat Fayaq Rahman*


You do not die! Not when you want to.
Not when you see your strong husband, the big
brother in his own family, kicked bloody by a group
of men equipped with loaded guns and hatred.

157

Not when your beautiful teenage daughter
is handpicked by soldiers, never comes back.
And for the rest of your life you are left to wonder:
was she sold to prostitution? Does she still live?

Not when your son withers in your lap
and he cries until he can no more, when the last thing
he asks of you is 'cucumber', and you give him
a green slipper to suckle on, because he is beyond

knowing the difference. No. Not even when
the rest of your children grow fed up with
your black garments, secret tears, headaches
when you smell cucumber. You do not die.


## Dispute Over a Mass Grave


The one you have finished examining
is my son. That is the milky coloured Kurdish
suit his father tailored for him, the blue shirt
his uncle gave to him. Your findings prove
that it is him – he was a tall fifteen year old,
was left handed, had broken a rib.

I know she too has been looking for her son
but you have to tell her that this is not him.
Yes the two of them were playmates and fought
the year before. But it was my son who broke
a rib, hers only feigned to escape trouble.

That one is mine! Please give him back to me.
I will bury him on the verge of my garden –
the mulberry tree will offer him its shadow,
the flowers will earnestly guard his grave,
the hens will peck on his gravestone,
the beehive will hum above his head.

# NICK MAKOHA

## King of Myth

Back when you were taken from our lives like
the son of God ascending into heaven at the barricade
to another life, policemen on their motorbikes
named you King of Myth. You danced to tossed grenades,
All part of the charade in their fire ritual. In a restless air
we surrendered our weapons – axe heads, shanks, short rope,
blades, some poison and all its animal understanding – now fair
game to the enemy with our world in their scope.
They came down hills during the blackout, phantoms
from a fallen sky with years of practice at soft landings
onto roofs in darkness, like a spirit slipping into skin.
The voice of their guns kept the violence from escaping.
A disturbance in the trees is easily mistaken for wind.
*Honey I'm still free, take a chance on me* – as the radio sings.

## Black Death

Two men who have never had a country of their own
fall out over a girl in a bar. In place of war they pull off their shirts,
lunatics in an embrace, as a barmaid fills my glass with local ale.

Policemen hang out of armed cars with sophisticated weapons.
Fleas fry on their backs as a ricochet gives voice to the air.
At full stretch a camera blinks at an unshaven male, clearly dead.

They are beating his body while I stand outside myself.
A year from now I will suffer the same death by water.
This body will be a map in the dark, moving towards a shore.

By the open stove of my wife's village there will be death by surprise,
death by marriage, death by having rummaged into the past,
into the distant past of a man that neither of us remembers.

After boycott marches there will be death by placards.
In radio silence Israeli ground troops will storm a home
looking for the Archbishop. Death by Judas kiss.

Lizard-coloured helicopters filled with embassy-men and snipers
with walkie talkies will signal  for death by longshot. Demonstrators
behind masks with eyes like loaded dice will ask for death by decay,

the body turning black, bloodlet like a pig. The crowd is here
offering false compliments to an immigrant on his knees.
Death by confession – words that are not your own.

A note whispered in earshot of a *New York Times* news crew
as man sets fire to himself. The body now an animal bent double
a shadow of vague form promising to raise itself from the earth.

VAHNI CAPILDEO

## About the Shape of Things

'Help me cut the world up
into paper shapes!
Then I'll know I see it.
Really.
I see it really.
Give things their names!'

     Nameless Bones Nameless Bones below oceans
     Nameless Bones we name them  That's all the names
     we have for you. The theme of everyone
     is Nameless Bones, ashamed or not to join
     in singing sea and nameless bones. Not for:
     Display. Arraignment. Arrangement. We're done.

And this morality of nameless bones
begins to stir in me against my will
to help – each flight home, every holiday,
layered by plane wings flouting nameless bones
while flickering with kinship, whispering
metal fatigue, systems' untimeliness,
the gentle letdown of oxygen masks,
profound and pressured sunless corals,
indifferent to excess of history –
against my will to help the namer. 'Why
I love the radiance that names bring, arrayed
corolla-like – ' 'Does it need signalling,
the central secret of each thing?' 'But yes,
as every secret we rejoice in. Say – '

Guyana's poet,
Martin Carter, said it:
*Till I collect my scattered skeleton...*

## HANNAH LOWE

## Borderliner

I'm skirting the bold lines of the map **border-liner, might mean white girl**
neither here nor there, but home in the border places **with corkscrew hair**
Tijuana, where rich American boys slam tequila **or brown girl with flat hair**
or controlled drugs, or down the fence **slipping from one side to the other**
where a veiled woman clutches her baby **always looking for the right light**
in the thin shadows **Passing, hoping the old world wouldn't catch her up**
always waiting to cross a *good day* or *hey girl* **in the wrong hotel or store**
I've always loved sea-swimming **some fool too loud, not seeing the signs**
but sometimes these waves carry **That kind of stuff could put you back in**
make-shift rafts bobbing empty of their cargo **chains or end with the blade**
below my feet, the sea-bed **but ever notice how green eyes in yellow skin**
cross-hatched with bones **look so good, how some faces have no borders**
There were times when these borders had **no fixed abode? You can sketch**
no barbed wire, and even now not all borders are **a pretty rainbow diagram**
so hard. There are places nobody cares to pass **or use faux scientific words**
Think of that frozen mountain trail where only a tin sign **to classify, or slang**
tells one snowy Nordic edge from another, or miles **relating to nation states**
of rough green march-lands **chocolate bars or animals – mongrel or mule**
where I have wandered for days **But I say it's only when you are standing**
That I'm home on the border doesn't mean **on the border that you are free**
I don't think about who took the world and carved it up **to look both ways**

# MATTHEW SHENODA

## Song of the Dispersed

Who put the hammer and the hoe in the hands of the poor?
THIRD WORLD, FREEDOM SONG


And there was a moment when things began to break

Even the cracked earth bears water

But that moment was not enough
has never served as salve for chaffed hands

And not because we are greedy
but because we are here
because we have been here
toiling

Not for recognition
but survival

And we can only speak of distance

When all of the bounty comes from a distant land
even the seed knows no home

And the heart of a cancerous man
shrinks oceans
just as the ringing ear of a child
finds music in the sky

And we continue our labor, knowing
that in the sordid steps of history
the staircase plays favorites

And they talk and talk and talk
but we know for the verbose
even the river creates anxiety

Just as when the rain falls
the thickness of the clouds is an illusion

Just as on the ringed finger of a man
all possibility is enshrined

And if our tongues were made of silt
nothing would die when we speak

And if each of us was named for possibility

the earth would harbor less cement

The axle of history
greased by blood and amazement

And the power of memory
existing in the history of death

Death, the resurrection
of memory

But we know virtually nothing of this history
only that it makes us whole

## The Unlearning

> And if we should live up in the hills.
>
> BURNING SPEAR

Death comes to us,
a shadow of itself.

Death, at the hands of the state.
Death, so often.
Death, so African.
Death, ancestry.
Black death.

A death that does not happen
in a foreign language.

Babylon system.
       Vampire.
Wrapping its growing hands
around the larynx of a man.

       But Babylon cannot have our children.

Babylon cannot conqueror bond,
cannot take the memory from a mother
or the sting from a father.

*Oh Obadiah Obadiah*
*Jah Jah sent us to catch vampire.*\*

An incantation sung for the marauders.

A trail that leads to warmth.
A synesthetic in the bush.
A man up in the hills.

       Babylon cannot have our children.

A prism in the wings of a hummingbird
ruby-throated
a flash to carry the moment
a reminder of the fleeting colors
inhabiting our lives.

So we find a place of stillness
hold our staff like the flag of tomorrow
and chant:

*Iron like a lion in Zion.*

And in these hills
the unlearning.
The maroon.
The marronage from senseless death.

Another century
& it remains the same.

The man in the hills
his head to the ground
hears the reverberations
from the whale at sea.

Her sonic song rippling from
ocean to shore
to the center of this volcanic mass.

Up through the earth,
this earth,
a reminder that the journey to the hills
has always been a journey from death.

\* Lyrics from Ketch Vampire written by Devon Irons, music by Lee Scratch Perry

# DEGNA STONE

## Of Mutuality

Look down at your hand,
the colour of your skin,
now imagine it was *other* –
whatever *other* means.

Watch the pigment rise (or fade),
feel the texture of your hair change,
blink the ache from eyes
refocusing in their new shade.

*How does the world look now?*

This happened in a flash
but a prickling sensation lingers.
This is not an abstract,
in a real sense there is no going back.

You've been holding your breath,
breathe out, this panic won't help.
Find someone who looks like
you used to, let your lives intersect.

*What will you do now, in your new skin?*

RISHI DASTIDAR

## On Board the 'Tynesider'

*On 13 November 1967, Martin Luther King travelled to Newcastle,*
*to be awarded an honorary doctorate by Newcastle University.*


All those hours in his study,
writing, crafting, polishing,
learning, rehearsing – until it
sounded like history spoke through
him, change spoke through him,
like God bent on fixing His mistakes
all at once spoke through him.

But actually he was at his best
when he was harried, harassed –
by time as well as the times –
at 1am on a slow train to somewhere
he would never go again, minting
coin we still spend in the realm
of hope as easily as he breathed.

RIGOBERTO GONZALEZ

## A Brief History of Fathers Searching for Their Sons

There once was a man who traveled by boat
to arrive on Montezuma's soil. Not explorer
or conqueror but a father who had carried his grief
from China. His son had made that trip to Big

Lusong a decade earlier but he disappeared among
the marigolds – the bursts of rage and rifle fire
in Torreón. But the man believed his son
was still alive and so began his search. Just

like the man who followed the coast
from Chiapas to San Diego, looking for
his wide-eyed boy who had joined the revolution.
The Mexican war had come to end but not

the stories of the men who left their
tiny villages for worlds much larger than
their fathers had informed them. But how
do itinerant sons meet their fates?

On the night the shopkeeper stayed up late
to watch the glow on the horizon coming
closer. So the rumors were true: the soldiers
were pillaging the dreams of the foreign-born.

No time to regret not heading north
to the mountain made of gold, where men
like him weren't welcomed anyhow. But now
this. Now hoof. Now bullet. Now final bow.

The youngest soldier in the cavalry felt
his face grow warmer as his target's shirt
grew redder as the cries of panic mixed with
the frenzied cries of victory. What misery

befell los chinos de Coahuila on that night
when their adoptive country chewed her
insides out. The headline's odor drifted to towns
along the border. When the Asian populations

shrunk, the Norteños joked that they had sunk
into that hole dug to China. The headline's shriek
then reached the shore of Mexico by way of the man
gone mad, who had swallowed the scream

of the man he had shot and so he was cursed
to repeat that sound until he threw himself
into the sea. *I kept his suffering soul but I pushed
his body back to the deserted beach. I didn't want*

*that much sadness inside of me*, said the sea.
And that was the end of that until two other
men came to ask the great ocean, great witness
of triumphs and tragedies, if it had come

upon their sons. Question spoken one hundred times
before. Question to be spoken one hundred times
more. But this was an occasion the sea had never
seen: the father of a son who had killed a man

crossing paths with the slain man's father.
How they comforted each other knowing
they were not alone on their journey.
How they accepted consolation not knowing

about that terrible connection between
their sons. And that's why the sea kept quiet.
For even gods capable of fury can temper
their waters for a temporary taste of mercy.

But silence too has a price: blindness. The fathers
exchanged nods and moved on – one heading
north, the other heading east, both energised
by the encounter with another man

who loved his son so fully he couldn't
lose him to uncertainty. Call it folly, it's
the history of migration: life granting men
such cravings for adventure, curiosity, purpose

and ambition, their stories pass each other by
without notice, or collide – a strike that's
fatal, or inexplicably polite. What decides
if the outcome is heartache or glory?

*Don't look at me, says the sea. I too shift up
and down, back and forth. Even I don't know
where I'm going, how the journey will be. I'm
no less immigrant than you, no more the refugee.*

## MALIKA BOOKER

## Faithful

you in the market square, hair matted brillo;
a nest of brambles, feet caked with road dirt.

you in faded blue dress, tear and rip patterned
dust caked till next sea bathe, till next rain shower,

till next meal of raw fish and bin food. you with ears
for walking stick, yesterday you heard his voice preach

and you became a snail sliding on belly to touch his hem,
how many times you ears deceive and you hands claw

space, reach like a babies hand stretched to grab bottle.
and when you touched his hem you hold on and beg *release me*.

## Broken Gifts

we the lonely sit at bus shelters or on train seats
our bodies seeking to purge our aching black bags

into a strangers ear like they signed on these journeys
as shrinks to be burdened by mouths spinning cobwebs,

last night slumped in the witness stand of my dream
I was asked, *who teaches our black girls to receive praise*

*like lotion, then rub it tenderly into their skin*, as hundreds
of Nigerian girls flooded the court room like moths

filling empty fields with their brittle wings and despair
seeking their mothers among the strangers in this room.

ADA LIMÓN

## A New National Anthem

The truth is, I've never cared for the National
Anthem. If you think about it, it's not a good
song. Too high for most of us with 'the rockets
red glare' and then there are the bombs.
(Always, always, there is war and bombs.)
Once, I sang it at homecoming and threw
even the tenacious high school band off key.
But the song didn't mean anything, just a call
to the field, something to get through before
the pummeling of youth. And what of the stanzas
we never sing, the third that mentions 'no refuge
could save the hireling and the slave'? Perhaps,
the truth is, every song of this country
has an unsung third stanza, something brutal
snaking underneath us as we blindly sing
the high notes with a beer sloshing in the stands
hoping our team wins. Don't get me wrong, I do
like the flag, how it undulates in the wind
like water, elemental, and best when it's humbled,
brought to its knees, clung to by someone who
has lost everything, when it's not a weapon,
when it flickers, when it folds up so perfectly
you can keep it until it's needed, until you can
love it again, until the song in your mouth feels
like sustenance, a song where the notes are sung
by even the ageless woods, the short-grass plains,
the Red River Gorge, the fistful of land left
unpoisoned, that song that's our birthright,
that's sung in silence when it's too hard to go on,
that sounds like someone's rough fingers weaving
into another's, that sounds like a match being lit
in an endless cave, the song that says my bones
are your bones, and your bones are my bones,
and isn't that enough?

## ROWAN RICARDO PHILLIPS

## The Once and Future King of Ohio

Dawn. Two roosters stud the side of the road.
One of them is dead. The other stands there
Stiff in the car's sudden breeze, staring out
Across the hilly Ohio highway,
Skyward towards that something slight of bright
Reds and pinks, a pallid rooster-feathered
Hue, as silent as the rooster standing
And as distant as the rooster on its side.
We drove by, my guide and I, too quickly
To know if one rooster was waiting for
The other, or which had been waiting—,
Or, if they'd planned to cross the road together
When suddenly something went terribly wrong
Either at the end of having crossed it
Or simply, as happens, during the wait.

The whole Ohio highway seemed to know, though,
Like the gate of Heaven you see at death
(As a light or a shining shunning darkness)
Knows Heaven without actually being
Heaven, being rather just a border,
Still part of our plausible world
Of parts, living and dead, male and female,
Color and color, belief and belief...
There's really no reason to believe or
Not to believe what you see when you see it.
But when at speed I saw those two roosters
Trying to figure out what's next for them
As the distances we travelled on the
661 swallowed them whole with wheat,
I looked from my passenger's seat into
The car's rearview mirror, and saw nothing
That was neither Heaven nor Ohio
As the horses stirred, and the steeples slept,
And the state flattened out like a mirror.
And am I not a mirror for that mirror?

174

# NATALIE DIAZ

## American Arithmetic

Native Americans make up less than
one percent of the population of America.
0.8 percent of 100 percent.

O, mine efficient country.

I do not remember the days
before America – I do not remember the days
when we were all here.

Police kill Native Americans more
than any other race. *Race* is a funny word,
*Race* implies someone will win,
implies *I have as good a chance of winning as –*

Who wins the race which isn't a race?

Native Americans make up 1.9 percent
of all police killings, higher than any race,
and we exist as .8 percent of all Americans.

Sometimes *race* means *run*.

We are not good at math.
Can you blame us?
We've had an American education.

We are Americans and we are less than 1 percent
of Americans. We do a better job of dying
by police than we do existing.

When we are dying, who should we call?
The police? Or our senator?
Please, someone, call my mother.

In Arithmetic and in America,
divisibility has rules –
divide without remainder.

At the National Museum of the American Indian,
68 percent of the collection is from the U.S.
I am doing my best to not become a museum
of myself. I am doing my best to breathe in and out.

I am begging: *Let me be lonely but not invisible.*

But in this American city with all its people,
I am Native American – less than one, less than
whole – I am less than myself. Only a fraction
of a body, let's say, *I am only a hand* –

and when I slip it beneath the shirt of my lover
I disappear completely.

## Manhattan is a Lenape Word

*from the ACE Hotel, Midtown*

It is December, and we must be brave.

The ambulance's rose of light
blooming against the window.
Its single siren-cry: *Help me.*
A silk-red shadow moving like water
through the orchard of her thigh.

Her, come – in the green night, a lion.
I sleep her bees with my mouth of smoke,
dip honey with my hands sweetened
on the dark and hive of her breast.
Out of the eater I eat. Meaning,
*She is mine, colony.*

The things I know aren't always easy:
I'm the only Native American
on the 8th floor of this hotel or any,
looking out any window
of a turn-of-the-century building
in Manhattan. *Manhattan* is
a Lenape word.

Even a watch must be wound.
How can a century or a heart turn
if nobody asks, *Where have all
the natives gone?*

If you are where you are, then where
are those who are not here? Not here.
Which is why in this city I have
many lovers. All my loves
are reparations loves.

What is loneliness if not unimaginable
light and measured in lumens –
an electric bill which must be paid,
a taxi cab floating across three lanes
with its lamp lit, gold in wanting.
At 2 a.m. everyone in New York City
is empty and asking for someone.

Again, the siren's same wide note:
*Help me.* Meaning, *I have a gift
and it is my body*, made two-handed
of gods and bronze.

She says, *You make me feel
like lightning.* I say, *I don't ever
want to make you feel that white.*
It's too late – I can't stop seeing
her bones. I'm counting the carpals,
metacarpals of her hand
when she is inside me.

One bone, the lunate bone, is named
for its crescent outline, lunatus, luna.
Some nights she rises like that in me,
like trouble – a slow, luminous, flux.

The moon beckons the lonely
coyote wandering West 29th Street
by offering its long wrist of light.
The coyote answers by lifting its head
and crying stars.

Somewhere far from New York City,
an American drone finds then loves
a body – the glowing nectar it seeks
through great darkness – makes
a candle-hour of it, and burns
gently along it, like American touch,
an unbearable heat.

The siren song returns in me,
I sing it across her throat: Am I
what I love? Is this the glittering world
I've been begging for?

# ARACELIS GIRMAY

## *from* The Black Maria

*After Neil deGrasse Tyson, black astrophysicist & director of the Hayden Planetarium, born in*
*1958, New York City. In his youth, deGrasse Tyson was confronted by police on more than one*
*occasion when he was on his way to study stars.*

I've known that I've wanted to do astrophysics since I was nine years old, a
first visit to the Hayden Planetarium... So I got to see how the world around
me reacted to my expression of these ambitions. & all I can say is, the fact that
I wanted to be a scientist, an astrophysicist, was, hands down, the path of most
resistance... Anytime I expressed this interest teachers would say, Don't you
want to be an athlete? Or, Don't you wanna... I wanted to become something
that was outside of the paradigms of expectation of the people in power. And I
look behind me and say, Well, where are the others who might have been this?
And they're not there. And I wonder, What is the [thing] along the tracks
that I happened to survive and others did not? Simply because of the forces
that prevented it. At every turn. At every turn.

NEIL DEGRASSE TYSON, The Center for Inquiry, 2007

*Body of space. Body of dark.*
*Body of light.*

The Skyview apartments
          circa 1973, a boy is
kneeling on the rooftop, a boy who
          (it is important
to mention here his skin
          is brown) prepares his telescope,
the weights & rods,
          to better see the moon. His neighbor
(it is important to mention here
          that she is white) calls the police
because she suspects the brown boy
          of something, she does not know
what at first, then turns,
          with her white looking,
his telescope into a gun,
          his duffel into a bag of objects
thieved from the neighbors' houses

179

(maybe even hers) & the police
(it is important to mention
        that statistically they
are also white) arrive to find
        the boy who has been turned, by now,
into 'the suspect', on the roof
        with a long, black lens, which is,
in the neighbor's mind, a weapon &
        depending on who you are, reading this,
you know that the boy is in grave danger,
        & you might have known
somewhere quiet in your gut,
        you might have worried for him
in the white space between lines 5 & 6,
        or maybe even earlier, & you might be holding
your breath for him right now
        because you know this story,
it's a true story, though,
        miraculously, in this version
of the story anyway,
        the boy on the roof of the Skyview lives
to tell the police that he is studying
        the night & moon & lives
long enough to offer them (the cops) a view
        through his telescope's long, black eye, which,
if I am spelling it out anyway,
        is the instrument he borrowed
& the beautiful 'trouble' he went through
        lugging it up to the roof
to better see the leopard body of
        space speckled with stars & the moon far off,
much farther than (since I am spelling *The Thing*
        out) the distance between
the white neighbor who cannot see the boy
        who is her neighbor, who,
in fact, is much nearer
        to her than to the moon, the boy who
wants to understand the large
        & gloriously un-human mysteries of
the galaxy, the boy who, despite 'America',
        has not been killed by the murderous jury of

his neighbor's imagination & wound. This poem
        wants only the moon in its hair & the boy on the roof.
This boy on the roof of this poem
        with a moon in his heart. Inside my own body
as I write this poem my body
        is making a boy even as the radio
calls out the Missouri coroner's news,
        the Ohio coroner's news.
2015. My boy will nod
        for his milk & close his mouth around
the black eye of my nipple.
        We will survive. How did it happen?
The boy. The cops. My body in this poem.
        My milk pulling down into droplets of light
as the baby drinks & drinks them down
        into the body that is his own, see it,
splayed & sighing as a star in my arms.
        Maybe he will be the boy who studies stars.
Maybe he will be (say it)
        the boy on the coroner's table
splayed & spangled
        by an officer's lead as if he, too, weren't made
of a trillion glorious cells & sentences. Trying to last.


Leadless, remember? The body's beginning,
splendored with breaths, turned,
by time, into, at least, this song.
This moment-made & the mackerel-'soul'
caught flashing inside the brief moment of the body's net,
then, whoosh, back into the sea of space.

The poem dreams of bodies always leadless, bearing
only things ordinary
as water & light.

# SANDEEP PARMAR

### *from* Eidolon

#### XLIX

Let us be as a city upon a hill
        as a stone or several stones
        as white shells in each city's layer
                – each layer a memorable human hour –
                        gathering the sea and all its warble in the dust.

If you roll into LA from the East
by car           by road through oaks and sycamores
that give way to studio lots
        barred up like penitentiaries
            dreams assembled stone by stone
            behind a forbidding wall wreathed by wire

If you enter from the air
descending through smog      its brown meniscus
watch the city light up
        like a motherboard on high alert
        from the dry sanctuary between Vegas and mountain ranges
The bric-a-brac of cacti      the desert lore of cannibalism
and invisible tribes of off-the-gridsmen
rattling tinnily in the ears         of cascading Sierras

Let us be as a city
        on the stones of other cities

Troy dignified and silent
        draws a stratified cloak of nine kingdoms
        over its brittle shoulders
Its cape of stone      has been smoothed by the humble footfall
of its slaves and women.

Stop and listen
as you stand high on its brow          hear the hot wind
         rush up the hillsides of brush
through some sort of oak (we think).


We collect its seeds
to plant a Troy-tree
in our Californian garden.
         [My mother, convinced it will live.
Unlike the pomegranate, fruitless, wanting
some eternal myth denied by the Pacific.
Biblical fruit, sole comfort of the dead, its globules of ruby life –
613 cells of blood that pour
in the Babylonian crush
of idle days and endless cruelties,
no, it will not grow on my mother's lawn
in an exile's confusion of lavender,
red marigold and lily flower.]


Mother, let us be as a city, rising
         not swept through
                  by the greed of rumoured enemies.


If you arrive by boat to Troy
through quietest midnight       in the pre-blue of black
         slipping in the tide past Lemnos
abrupt on the horizon
you will see the sun erupt
from behind a panorama of cloud


lighted scenes of warring gods
         burning in their silhouettes
                  the carnage that burnishes gold
                           scattered without excessive
                                    note over the Trojan plain.

# Mother Britain

This mother is a Briton colonising the alien attributes of her marriage; her marriage the appropriation of an alien property. [...] These so unserviceable rooms are her dominions; just so much of her grandure [sic]. The higgledy piddled[y] contents of the cupboards her national [reserves] [she] guards it and gloats to herself [...]

MINA LOY, 'Goy Israels'

This is not your England. Budgering the mind blank through millstone and wheelgrease, the typecast cast in bronze launch arrowheads or bear an alien wind to set your house alight. High gates and low grates for the ungracious. Mother Britain, the savages are coming with their kowtow indolence, to suffer your cream teas. Put them back in the foundries, before they develop a taste for it. You should have boiled them in oil on the white cliffs of Dover. Mother, you are stuck here – the television antennae, a boy in a paddock waving at the passing train, the edges of tabloid newspapers, they hook themselves around your knees. No, this is not your England. That turgid arteriole of cars running North to South, breeding a slow choke on the greenbelt in satellite town after town. No neighbourly smile awaits you there in Luton; that isn't England anymore for all the Pakistanis hobbling about with waxen faces, avoiding your bonfires by averting their eyes. Still, let us consider a lively Southall Diwali – how the natives drag their goat tails round in dances to amuse the supperers at The Brilliant, smiling, at you, their Lady in roses and lace, the waiters memsahibing kormas in small brass cauldrons. *Clever little girl! Little Indian!* Little wonder you love the Jolly Golly, clowning an impossible grin of sugar cubes in swollen lips, that is, until he puts his hand out for a tip. Or picks up his whip and drives you screaming to the foaming Tiber to drown yourself in better eras gone. Florals are in, so are heavy nightgowns, pregnancy, one-egg cake recipes, austerity measures of gin. Weren't you all drinking it in secret, carrying on in private, then popping out to the front gate, to wave at buses of schoolchildren? Baking in triplicate with shredded suet, offal and sweetmeats, pies acrid with uric kidneys, passed through dead fingertips into flour and salt and milk. That was your England. Before the duggard folly of old women in raincoats and round-heeled shoes, before the tally of empty houses was a childhood trick, before you could remember the sound of rationed foods entering the kitchen, before the socks of the grammar school girls shone like fresh paint you were born into a dying England. Mother, in 1915 the British Raj culled Sikh protesters and hung them all like dogs – what do you think of that? That slight shoves you off the sidewalk now, makes you redundant, marries your sons. Would it interest you to know that my grandmother, a pious wealthy

184

of Lahore, refused England's green shores lest the shadow of a gentile fall on her? The thought of you turned her stomach, of you and your beloved Queen. So have your hog roasts, your EDL marches, your reptile glances and polite prejudices, your charity balls, your 50s revival tableware, your tea-towel-suck-up-to-the-Royal-Wedding, your eleventh-hour cocktails and heraldic silver teaspoons – the embers of your Empire swallowed whole like red coals by the exceeding ex-dominions. Your wellie-wanging contests. Your 'spot the German'. Your blasted England.

LAUREN K. ALLEYNE

## Martin Luther King Jr Mourns Trayvon Martin

For you, son,
I dreamed a childhood
unburdened by hate;
a boyhood of adventure –
skinned knees and hoops,
first loves and small rebellions;
I dreamed you whole
and growing into your own
manhood, writing its definitions
with your daily being.
I dreamed you alive, living.

For you, America's African heir,
I dreamed a future
of open doors, of opportunity
without oppression,
of affirmation and action,
I dreamed Oprah and Obama
I dreamed Colin and Condoleezza
I dreamed doctors and dancers,
lawyers and linebackers, models,
musicians, mechanics, preachers
and professors and police, authors,
activists, astronauts, even,
all black as Jesus is.

I dreamed you dapper –
the black skin of you
polished to glow; your curls,
your kinks, your locs,
your bald, your wild,
your freshly barbered –
all beautiful.

I dreamed you wearing whatever the hell you want
and not dying for it.

For you, brother,
I dreamed a world softened
by love, free from the fear
that makes too-early ancestors of our men;
turns our boys into targets,
headlines, and ghosts.

I had a dream
*that my children will one day live*
*in a nation where they will not be judged*
*by the color of their skin*
*but by the content of their character.*
Sweet song of my sorrow.
Sweet dream, deferred.
For you, gone one, I dreamed
justice – her scales tipped
away from your extinction,
her eyes and arms unbound
and open to you
at last.

## Heaven?

*(for Sandra Annette Bland)*

Where does a black girl go
when her body is emptied
of her? And her wild voice,
where does it sing its story
when the knots of history
make a grave of her throat?
What of her future, blue-
broken, unmade? Her name,
– say it! – Sandra, unhoused;
her dreams and memories
lost to their source. Where

does a black girl's love go
when her heart is snapped
shut like a cell door, the key
out of reach as any justice?
And what gift is lost when
a black girl is made a body,
her light dimmed into shadow,
gone? How many angels weep
when a black girl is torn
into wings?

## Elegy
*(for Tamir)*

This was going to be a curse poem –
me hexing the man who ghosted you,
slivering his days into two-second
increments of agony. I began writing
the playground you could make of his body,
surfing his blood, making monkey bars
of his ribs, dancing his heart's rhythm
on his neck – an inexhaustible mischief,
an incorrigible spirit of boy let loose
in the white country of the murderer's
unshielded body. I would wish him dead,
but I want him nowhere near the realm
he exiled you to, so instead I composed
a soundtrack for his nightmares, a mixtape
of your laugh/the gurgle of your blood
exiting the wound he gave you/a festival
of sirens/your sister's scream/bang/repeat.
This, I understand, is the grief talking.
This is the unchained melody of rage.
But to write his haunting is to name you
hell and you have been misnamed enough,
sweet boy. I make of these words an altar,
instead. I breathe this poem into a prayer,
each syllable a taper burning in memory

of you. Sweet boy, let me build you here
a new body, radiantly black, limber, poised
to become its most beautiful becoming.
Let it be spirited with starsong and rich
with tomorrows. Let me make you a life-
time of days honeyed with love: feast.
You are safe here. Let me write you
again into your name, *Tamir*, baptise
you with tongue and tears. *Tamir. Tamir.*
Let me write you a black boy's heaven,
where freedom is a verb conjugated
by your being, where your only synonym
is beloved, blessed, child of the universe.
Instead, I imagine you there, beginning.

# ZAFFAR KUNIAL

## Poppy

Who crops up wherever ground is opened, broken…
No, this is not enough.

Who crops up where acidic ground is neutralised – in Belgium
blasted bones and rubble added their twist of lime
turning the disturbed earth red…
No, this is not enough.

Then where seeds lay buried, dormant – those older than I am,
catching light, can stir from their long sleep in time,
like history, raising a hand, a head…
No, this is not enough.

Remember? Who's there in the first script, on a Mesopotamian
tablet: *Hul* and *Gil* – 'joy flower' – a cuneiform
cocktail, our earliest remedy…

Who begot war in China, was named by Arabs *Abou-el-noum*,
'father of sleep'; a bloody sign of love's martyrdom –
*gul-e-lala* – 'flower of red', in Persian and Urdu…

Remember? Beloved of Persephone; also found in the tomb –
like a watch, worn on the wrist – of Tutankhamun,
and on coins issued by Herod…
No, this is not enough.

You need more? … Who crops up, fringing the banks of Lethe
after Troy; who bridges forgetfulness and memory,
life and death, relief and pain…

Who was loved by Coleridge who wished: that I could wrap up the view
from my house in a pill of opium and send it to you – to be
seen, swallowed, whole again…
No, this is not enough.

Who was the *minded flower* Shakespeare partly saw, in all the drowsy
syrups of the world – a release from grief that calls for more
far-fetched relief, and, as morphine,

sent your sap through my mother's veins, while she still could hear me,
while warmth remained in those hands that first held me,
first calmed my small, fevered brain...
No, this is not enough.

Whose pupil is a void dilating with light, its first and last entry –
a compound eye, in whichever form – who sees
the black dot of the beginning...

Who's there on that date when all the 1s meet, looped in a wreath
year upon year, or poked through the eye
of a buttonhole. There. I'm done...
No, this is not enough.

Then: *Mother* – *Mother* – last word of that bleeding, wrecked soldier,
as heard by the last Tommy, the last link to living memory –
spoken for now, like the countless millions

of mouthless dead. There in the underworld. The fallen, heavy
head. The deaths we live with. Enough said. Remember?
This is you. Wake up. You're summoned

No, this is not enough.

# Spider Trees, Pakistan

> During the early 1850s, it sometimes seemed as if the British and the
> Mughals lived not only in different mental worlds, but almost in different
> time zones.
>
> WILLIAM DALRYMPLE, *The Last Mughal*

English mists in subcontinental sun;
the withered veil at Miss Havisham's House;
think of that thought in the brain of John Donne
scrawling *In that the world's contracted thus*;
think of holding-spells catching up with time
the way snow floods the sky in slow suspension;
think, though it's a stretch, like shock-haired Einstein
wedding time and space as lacework tension...

With floods in Sindh, and their tenants long stranded,
these trees are warped globes, veiled spectres of silk.
It's these photos that have me, stretched, extended –
glued to a webpage since opening a link –
racking my brain for lines to catch how they carry
the gravities of home. Worlds I can't marry.

ROSS GAY

## A Small Needful Fact

Is that Eric Garner worked
for some time for the Parks and Rec.
Horticultural Department, which means,
perhaps, that with his very large hands,
perhaps, in all likelihood,
he put gently into the earth
some plants which, most likely,
some of them, in all likelihood,
continue to grow, continue
to do what such plants do, like house
and feed small and necessary creatures,
like being pleasant to touch and smell,
like converting sunlight
into food, like making it easier
for us to breathe.

## ILYA KAMINSKY

## We Lived Happily During the War

And when they bombed other people's houses, we

protested
but not enough, we opposed them but not

enough. I was
in my bed, around my bed America

was falling: invisible house by invisible house by invisible house.

I took a chair outside and watched the sun.

        In the sixth month
of a disastrous reign in the house of money

in the street of money in the city of money in the country of money,
our great country of money, we (forgive us)

lived happily during the war.

V

EDWARD DOEGAR

## Mens Rea

You must decide if it matters
What you make of these words
The context of this living hand
That rearranges a Rubik's cube

What I make of these words
Is a game of skill without risk
Like rearranging a Rubik's cube
To right what I made wrong

In a game of skill without risk
News won't stay news for long
To write what you read wrong
Could be the subject of this poem

News can stay news too long
The colour of those dead hands
Could be the subject of this poem
You must decide if it matters

# ISHION HUTCHINSON

## The Difference

They talk oil in heavy jackets and plaid over
their coffee, they talk Texas and the north cold,

but mostly oil and Obama, voices dipping
vexed and then they talk Egypt failing,

Greek broken and it takes cash for France not
charity and I rather speak Russia than Ukraine

one says in rubles, than whatever, whatever
the trouble, because there is sea and gold,

a tunnel, wherever right now, an-anyhow-Belarus,
oh, I will show you something, conspiring

coins, this one, China, and they marvel,
their minds hatched crosses, a frontier

zeroed not by voyage or pipeline nor the milk
foam of God, no, not the gutsy weather they talk

frizzled, the abomination worsening
opulence to squalor, never the inverse.

# SARAH HOWE

## Window

'It was clear that if Mr. Snowden was placed with a refugee family, this was the last place the government and the majority of Hong Kong society would expect him to be,' Mr Tibbo said. 'Nobody would look for him there.'

NEW YORK TIMES, September 7, 2016

these are good people he
says they won't turn you
in for a penny out in the
cold save for little acts of
kindness from foreigners
who know what it means
not to be able to go back-
ed into a corner in a state
-less to eat on every week
and still she gives this un-
named man the only bed

that fills up all but a few
sq ft in the last place any
one would look drawing
blinds he gulps down the
chicken nuggets explains
to a shy Filipino toddler
how they can beam lasers
through a closed window
that will turn a plastic cup
into a microphone and he
rattles the dice in his coke

## VIDYAN RAVINTHIRAN

## Our first house

we lost in months when the owners chose to sell.
To buy it ourselves was only improbable.
It's tough but we're luckier than many.
The mortgage would be reasonably unreasonable;
over the years we'd gradually find the money.
But in that area no one smiled at us;
we learned not to and to walk past quickly.
Every conversation with the neighbour
with whom we shared a wall and nothing else
was clenched as the talk of a stranger
trapped briefly in a lift with you or the aisle
of a packed train. We were the only renters.
The lads in their car yelled *Chopra* – racist, I suppose,
given his abysmal record for the Magpies.

## My parents and I

speak of the events which brought us here;
like bodies they pile up, the anecdotes. Later,
the electric toothbrush dies. One couldn't find a better
example of a 'first world problem'; though you'll remember
my thigh was burned once by a towel rail. It was torture.
But – suddenly – on the brink of my return
to my true home, the one in which we live
I touch the dry tome that lives on the cistern
– it's about our civil war – and feel as if
I could be anyone on this earth, or no one.
Except those gun-jostled in the lumbar curve
or dripped on through a shack of corrugated metal
or studying in cadjan huts by the weak glow of coconut oil
have no clean white space, do they, in which to shit.

# TARFIA FAIZULLAH

## Because There's Still a Sky, Junebug

I turn on the porchlight
so the insects *will* come,
so my skin that drank of you
can marvel at how
quickly it becomes enraged,
a luscious feast. I'm waiting
to hear myself crystallise
with revelation.
Who stands guard at rooms locked into tombs?
Who will dictate the order
in which we're consumed?
– I turn the light off,
but who taught me to stay quiet
when the power is down?
*You're so sweet*, men say to me,
but tonight, I want
no one. Tonight, a drone
in Yemen detonates and rends the sky,
and in my father's garden,
*drone* is a stingless bee unable
to make honey.
I crush the antennae, regard
the exoskeleton. Do we ever learn
that we're given weapons
to be vicious so we can be sweet?
I look up,
because there is still a sky, the junebug
that whirs across it, because
there is still a head-scarfed girl
who sucks the sugar
from a ginger candy
before she explodes – I look up,
and the sky still flints with so many stars. Above me.
Above you.

## I Told the Water

*(for Flint, MI)*

I told the water            You're right

      the poor are

           broken sidewalks

we try to avoid

Told it            the map of you folds into corners      small enough

      to swallow            I told the water

You only exist because of thirst

      But beside your sour membrane     we lie

         facedown in dirt

The first time            my father threw me into you

      I became hieroglyph           a wet braid

         caught       in your throat

I knew then            how *war* was possible

                the urge

to defy gravity       to dis-
           arm another

      I knew then we'd kill

to be your mirror       You   black-eyed barnacle

         You      graveyard

of windows           I told the water

      Last night I walked out onto the ice

              wearing only my skin

You couldn't tell me      not to

VALZHYNA MORT

## Singer

A yoke of honey in a glass of cooling milk.
Bats playful like butterflies on power lines.
In all your stories blood hangs like braids

of drying onions. Our village is so small,
it doesn't have its own graveyard. Our souls,
are sapped in sour water of the bogs.

Men die in wars, their bodies their graves.
And women burn in fire. When midsummer
brings thunderstorms, we cannot sleep

because our house is a wooden sieve,
and crescent lightning cut off our hair.
The bogs ablaze, we sit all night in fear.

I always thought that your old trophy Singer
would hurry us away on its arched back.
I thought we'd hold on to its mane of threads

from loosened spools along Arabic spine,
same threads that were sown into my skirts,
my underthings, first bras. What smell

came from those threads you had so long,
sown in, pulled out, sown back into the clothes
that held together men who'd fall apart

undressed. Same threads between my legs!
I lash them, and the Singer gallops!

And sky hangs only the lightning's thread.
Like in that poem: on Berlin's Jaegerstrasse
Arian whores are wearing shirts ripped off
sliced chests of our girls. My Singer-Horsey,

why everything has to be like that poem?

# MAI DER VANG

## Transmigration

Spirit, when I flee this jungle, you must too.
I will take our silver bars, necklace dowry, and the kettle
forged from metal scraps just after the last monsoon.

Among the foliage, we must be ready to see
the half-decayed. You must not run off no matter how much
flesh you smell.

Nor should you wander to chase an old mate.

Spirit, we arc in this with each other the way the night geese
in migration need the stars.

When I make the crossing, you must not be taken no matter what
the current gives. When we reach the camp,

there will be thousands like us.
If I make it onto the plane, you must follow me to the roads
and waiting pastures of America.

We will not ride the water today on the shoulders of buffalo
as we used to many years ago, nor will we forage
for the sweetest mangoes.

I am refugee. You are too. Cry, but do not weep.

We walk out the door.

# Faith in a time of double-dip recessions.

*– for those who pray for money.*

Once in the blue moon of my prayers,
I rise, brush the dust off my knees and
imagine the answering angel hears me
as Tiger Woods might sense a far hole:
such fields of folks, of distance to cover
and one stroke to get it right. The angel,

he floats down and with the featherest
of touches taps a bus driver's shoulder
vanishing in a puff of something warm
that smells like home. She turns, sniffs.
A sudden longing hits her gut. The bus
stalls for ten short seconds but it's long
enough for Ahmed to sulk off, hail a taxi,
ask the chatty driver politely to shut up
and drive. Down the road he accelerates
Got to get this bastard off my backseat
he thinks, narrowly missing Mrs Smith
who startles her latte across her blouse,
spews the foulest words. A school girl
passing taps her teacher with That's it!
Daddy used those words! Father calls,
cancels his afternoon mistress to meet
his daughter's teacher for a serious talk
and the angel grips his clipboard, ticks
the box for [ ] Sin Additionally Averted
as he catalogues the toppling dominoes
of his handiwork: that's us. Coiling out
across the city, the magnificent dance
of chance and chaos that few revel in,
many hate, some believe to be ordered
only when desperate, whispering Help,
intense, needing, as I, of money, love
or strength to break a door as a burglar

might when the alarm goes off and old
Miss Williams, arms laden with bin bags
outside the Job Centre where she works,
searches for keys, misses a five pound
note leak from her purse. It falls slow
as feathers, holy as answered prayers
to land among bags of reference letters,
CVs, job applications and exam results:
these littered like discarded dreams of
a generation; a new bag placed on top.

I imagine the angel planned all this, felt
I would step out empty handed, save a
couple pennies tinkling like false gods.
His left wing kinda twitched and he saw
I would come along, head bowed, feet
scuffing concrete, kick one plastic bag
swollen with rain, glimpse the five pound
note I scoop into the emptiness that is
my wallet, lift my voice past skyscrapers,
stars glittering with the mysterious ways
it's said he works in, on, past the angels
to finally thank God.


## Fragments of bone.


Let me begin again, I say, as the bar blurs
invisible, its volume reduced to the merest
suggestion of others and it's just us spotlit
in the black womb-like silence of theatre
and your question themes the play; let me
begin again: I went to church last Sunday.

The pastor preached: put not your faith in
man who only is good as his next breath;
align your faith with he who gives breath.
Here I stutter, my answer splintering like

fragments of bone against the mud soil
of memory. Moments before, I recalled

the call to prayer: In the Name of Allah
Most Gracious, Most Merciful – the slow
unfurling Imam's son's voice as dusk
touched the courtyard, the dust settling,
the sun solemnly bowed on the horizon –
thin as a prayer mat – and the gathered
performing ablutions: Bismillah, they say,
washing hands, mouths, nostrils, faces,
arms, head, ears, feet, kneeling to pray
Allah Is Great, God Is Great, they say.

You counter with airplanes, fireballs,
towers falling; stop your rant with
the first fireman to die, his skull caved
by a jumper from the 51st floor fleeing
flames. In the name of Allah, Gracious,
Great, Merciful this was done, you say.

I mention Amazing Grace, how sweet
the choir leader swayed in white robes,
eyes closed, humming southern baptist
hymn hypnotic, sailing congregations
to the oceanic depth whence his tears:
wide and sure as waves ride back and
forth that everything would be all right.

You rejected faith again, describing Jos,
Nigeria, the girl watching flat amongst
tall grass: the squad of Christian men
who hold her mother down as another
swings down with a machete, down as
sunlight skates the blade's edge, down,
the last swing, the fragments of bone
and there are screams no more.

There's blood in the drama of Men and
Gods, you say: rivers of it flow through
our wounded earth, gush from scripts

in houses of worship and act after act
aren't all stained? except the audience?
the secular astray? You gesture toward
those seated in darkness who gawk as we
squabble on stage; aren't they the ones
the light beyond will touch unbloodied?
who will die hands clean?

... Let me begin again, I say, I went to
church/the pastor preached/faith/man
/breath/... I stutter, the bar blurs back
to life, words falls against your ears.

## The N Word

### I

You sly devil. Lounging in a Pinter script
or pitched from a transit van's rolled-down window;
my shadow on this until road, though you've been
smuggled from polite conversation. So when
a friend of a friend has you poised on his lips
you are not what he means, no call for balled fist,
since he's only signifyin(g) on the sign;
making wine from the bad blood of history.
Think of how you came into my life that day,
of leaves strewn as I had never seem them strewn,
knocking me about the head with your dark hands.

### II

> Pretty little lighty but I can get dark
>
> MZ BRATT, 'Get Dark'

You came back as rubber lips, pepper grains, bilk
you're so black you're blik and how the word stuck to
our tongues eclipsing – or so we thought – all fear
that any moment anyone might notice
and we'd be deemed the wrong side of a night sky.
Lately you are *a pretty little lighty* who can
*get dark* because, even now, dark means street
which means beast which means leave now for Benfleet.
These days I can't watch a music video
online without you trolling in the comments,
dressed to kill in your new age binary clothes.

# Casting

My agent says I have to use my street voice.
Though my talent is for rakes and fops I'll drop
the necessary octaves, stifle a laugh
at the playwright's misplaced *get me blud* and *safe*.
If I get it they'll ask how long it takes me
to grow *cornrows* without the small screen's knowing
wink. Three years RADA, two years rep and I'm sick
of playing *lean dark men who may have guns*.
I have a book of poems in my rucksack,
blank pad, two pens, tattered A-Z, headphones
and know Prokofiev as well as Prince Paul.

RAYMOND ANTROBUS

## Two Days and Two Nights in Kisumu, Kenya

The world in English has sharp edges

BINYAVANGA WAINAINA

### Day 1

The classroom is an open-air hut,
84 children on chairs and low brick walls.
I walk in reeking of the road.
There's a gap in the roof where sunlight
beams onto my forehead.
*Hello*, I say. *Jambo Bwana*, the class says.
Dan, a Kenyan teacher, explains
the kids speak Luo and Kiswahili
so he will need to translate.
Even the poets I met in Cape Town
would call this village *the real Africa*
not because the children don't have shoes (they do)
but because there are no hotels
or British schools or Chinese Casinos.
Shannon, a girl in a faded Man United shirt
asks how I become a poet.
I start talking in a language distant
until Dan carries my story in his tongue.

### Night 1

Barack Obama is 'part-Kenyan' and has an 'ancestral' hatred of Britain

BORIS JOHNSON

I lie in the candlelit hut
thinking how English
would never be the right tongue
to ask this class what matters.
I wonder what if no European
discovered anything in Kenya?
What if there was no brutal history

210

to speaking and writing English?
Would they still have
colonised the classroom?

Ben

                John    David

                                  Christine       Hayley

     Toby

## Day 2

> We are more interested in the future than the past
>
> DAVID CAMERON on reparations for
> the Trans-Atlantic Slave Trade

After hearing Cameron on the radio
I dreamt of Uhuru Kenyatta refusing
to apologise for Africa's role in slavery
and under-developing Europe
because Africa is
*more interested in the future.*

I wake to say that even though I have come
to teach poetry, and not history, our language
has not come from the future, it has crawled
from a cave and rowed to so many shores
that we speak in crashed waves and trade winds.

## Night 2

> The problem is not that we were once in charge [in Africa] but that we are
> not in charge any more
>
> BORIS JOHNSON

Dan drives me to the airport
past Lake Victoria.
I ask him if he knows
the name of that lake
before 1858.
He says *I could tell you
but it has no meaning in English.*

## Jamaican British

*after 'Broken Ghazal' by Aaron Samuels*


Some people would deny that I'm Jamaican British.
Angelo nose. Hair straight. No way I can be Jamaican British.

They think I say I'm black when I say Jamaican British
but the English boys at school made me choose Jamaican, British?

Half-caste, half mule, house slave – Jamaican British.
Light skin, straight male, privileged – Jamaican British.

Eat callaloo, plantain, jerk chicken – I'm Jamaican
British don't know how to serve our dishes, they enslaved us.

In school I fought a boy in the lunch hall – Jamaican.
At home, told Dad *I hate dem, all dem Jamaicans* – I'm British.

He laughed, said *you cannot love sugar and hate your sweetness*,
took me straight to Jamaica – passport, British.

Cousins in Kingston called me Jah-English,
proud to have someone in their family – British.

Plantation lineage, World War service, how do I serve Jamaican British?
When knowing how to war is Jamaican
British.

# PUBLICATION ACKNOWLEDGEMENTS

The poems in this anthology are reprinted from the following books or journals, all by permission of the publishers listed unless stated otherwise. Thanks are due to all copyright holders stated below for their kind permission.

**John Agard:** 'Voice' from *Playing the Ghost of Maimonides* (Bloodaxe Books, 2016). **Elizabeth Alexander:** 'Praise Song for the Day', first read at Barack Obama's Presidential Inauguration, January 20, 2009, and published by Graywolf Press, by permission of Faith Childs Literary Agency on behalf of Elizabeth Alexander. **Lauren K. Alleyne:** 'Heaven?' was first published as Split This Rock Poem of the Week Friday, September 9, 2016, by permission of the author. **Moniza Alvi:** 'I Hold My Breath in This Country With Its Sad Past' from *Europa* (Bloodaxe Books, 2008); 'How the Children Were Born' and 'How the Stone Found Its Voice' from *Split World: Poems 1990-2005* (Bloodaxe Books, 2008). **Raymond Antrobus:** 'Jamaican British' and 'Two Days and Two Nights in Kisumu, Kenya' from *To Sweeten Bitter* (Out-Spoken Press, 2017), by permission of the author.

**James Berry:** 'In God's Greatest Country, 1945' and 'Travelling As We Are' from *A Story I Am In: New & Selected Poems* (Bloodaxe Books, 2011). **Kevin Bowen:** 'Dioxin Song' from *Eight True Maps of the West* (Dedalus Press, Dublin, 2003). 'About as Close as You Can Get' from the journal *Intervention*, 2002, by permission of the author. **Jean 'Binta' Breeze:** 'Aid Travels with a Bomb' from *Third World Girl: Selected Poems* (Bloodaxe Books, 2011).

**Vahni Capildeo:** 'About the shape of things' from *Dark & Unaccustomed Words* (Egg Box, 2012), by permission of the author. **Kayo Chingonyi:** 'The N Word' and 'Casting' from *Kumukanda* (Chatto & Windus, 2017), by permission of the author.

**Toi Derricotte:** 'On the Turning Up of Unidentified Black Female Corpses' from *Captivity*, by Toi Derricotte, © 1989. reprinted by permission of the University of Pittsburgh Press. **Rita Dove:** 'Freedom Ride' and 'Rosa' from *On the Bus with Rosa Parks*, W.W. Norton & Company, New York, NY. © 1999 by Rita Dove. 'Teach Us to Number Our Days' from *The Yellow House on the Corner*, W.W. Norton & Company, New York, NY. © 1980 by Rita Dove, reprinted by permission of the author. **Ian Duhig:** 'Croix-des-Bouquets, Haiti' and 'Fatras Baton' from *The Bradford Count* (Bloodaxe Books, 1991), by permission of the author. **Camille T. Dungy:** 'The Preachers Eat Out', 'Greyhound to Baton Rouge', and 'My Grandmother Takes the Youth Group to Services', from *What to Eat, What to Drink, What to Leave for Poison* (Red Hen Press, 2006), by permission of the author.

**Cornelius Eady:** 'Emmett Till's Glass Top Casket', 'Future Crimes' and 'The Blues', by permission of the author. **Inua Ellams:** 'Faith in a time of double-dip recessions – for those who pray for money' from *The Wire-headed Heathen* (Akashic Books, 2016), and 'Fragments of Bone' from *Candy Coated Unicorns and Converse All Stars* (Flipped Eye, 2011), by permission of the author. **Martín Espada:** 'How We Could Have Lived or Died This Way' from *Vivas to Those Who Have Failed* (W.W. Norton & Company, 2016); 'Sleeping on the Bus' from *Imagine the Angels of Bread* (W.W. Norton & Company, 1996); and 'Litany at the Tomb of Frederick Douglass' from *The Trouble Ball* (W.W. Norton & Company, 2011), by permission of the author.

**Tarfia Faizullah:** 'Because There's Still a Sky, Junebug' originally appeared in *Oxford American*, and 'I Told the Water' in *Michigan Quarterly Review*, by permission of the author. **Nikki Finnney:** 'Red Velvet' and 'My Time Up With You' from *Head Off and Split* (Evanston: TriQuarterly Books/Northwestern University Press, 2011), copyright © 2011 by Nikki Finney, published 2011 by TriQuarterly Books/Northwestern University Press, all rights reserved.

**Ross Gay:** 'A Small Needful Fact', originally appeared on *Split this Rock*, by permission of the author. **Aracelis Girmay:** Section I of *The Black Maria*, copyright © 2016 by Aracelis Girmay, by permission of The Permissions Company, Inc. on behalf of BOA Editions Ltd, www.boaeditions.org. **Nikki Giovanni:** 'In The Spirit of Martin' from *Chasing Utopia* (William Morrow, 2013), by permission of the author Nikki Giovanni © 2013.

**Marilyn Hacker:** 'Calligraphies III' originally appeared in *PN Review* and *Kenyon Review*, by permission of the author. **Choman Hardi:** 'Gas Attack', 'Dibs Camp, The Women's Prison' and 'Dispute Over a Mass Grave' from *Considering the Women* (Bloodaxe Books, 2015). **Jo Harjo**: 'No' from *Conflict Resolution for Holy Beings* (W.W. Norton, 2015), by permission of the author. **Kendel Hippolyte**: 'Poem in a Manger' from *Birthright* (Peepal Tree Press, 1997), by permission of the author. **Fanny Howe**: 'Heart Copy' and 'The Feast' by permission of the author. **Sarah Howe**: 'Window' written as part of a commission from Asia Art Archive called 'Six Windows'. **Ishion Hutchinson**: 'The Difference' from *House of Lords and Commons* (Farrar, Straus and Giroux, 2016), by permission of the author.

**Major Jackson**: 'Going to Meet the Man' from *Holding Company* (W.W. Norton & Company, 2010), 'Stand Your Ground' and 'On Disappearing' from *Roll Deep* (W.W. Norton & Company, 2015), by permission of the author. **Honorée Fanonne Jeffers**: 'Blues for Harpsichord, or, the Boston Massacre' and 'Mothering #2', by permission of the author. **Tyehimba Jess**: 'Against Silence' and 'Habeas Corpus', by permission of the author. **Linton Kwesi Johnson**: 'Reggae Fi Dada', by permission of the author.

**Ilya Kaminsky**: 'We Lived Happily During the War' from *Poetry International 2013* (Poetry International website, 2013), by permission of the author. **Mimi Khalvati**: 'Afterwardness' originally appeared in *PN Review*, by permission of the author. **Yusef Komunyakaa**: 'Our Side of the Creek' originally appeared in *Poetry*, 'Ota Benga at Edankraal' in *Poem-a-Day*, and 'The Soul's Soundtrack' in *The New Yorker*, by permission of the author. **Zaffar Kunial**: 'Poppy' and 'Spider Trees, Pakistan', by permission of the author.

**Ada Limón**: 'A New National Anthem', first published on BuzzFeed, 2 December 2016, by permission of the author. **Hannah Lowe**: 'Borderliner' from *Chan* (Bloodaxe Books, 2016).

**Mark McMorris**: 'Letter for K' from *Entrepôt* (2010), by permission of the author. **Nick Makoha**: 'King of Myth' and 'Black Death' from *Kingdom of Gravity* (Peepal Tree Press, 2017), by permission of the author. **Philip Metres**: 'Compline' and 'Testimony (after Daniel Heyman)' from *Sand Opera* (Alice James Books, 2015), by permission of the author.

**Daljit Nagra**: 'The Dream of Mr Bulram's English', from *British Museum* (Faber, 2017), by permission of the author. **Marilyn Nelson**: 'Boys in the Park' from *The Fields of Praise. New and Selected Poems* (LSU Press, 1997), by permission of LSU Press on behalf of Marilyn Nelson. **Grace Nichols**: 'A Brief Odyssey' from *The Insomnia Poems* (Bloodaxe Books, 2017).

**Gregory Pardlo**: 'Winter After the Strike, copyright © 2017, Gregory Pardlo, all rights reserved, by permission of the author. **Rae Paris**: 'To the Killers of Us' from *The Forgetting Tree: A Rememory* (Wayne State University Press, 2017), by permission of the author. **Sandeep Parmar**: XLIX from *Eidolon* (Shearsman, 2015), by permission of the publisher. **Carl Phillips**: 'Haloing the Lion', first published in *Fogged Clarity* (Winter 2015), by permission of the author. **Rowan Ricardo Phillips**: 'The Once and Future King of Ohio', first published in *Callaloo*, 37 no 2 (Spring 2014), and in *Heaven* (Farrar, Straus and Giroux), by permission of the author. **Robert Pinsky**: 'Poem of Disconnected Parts' from *Gulf Music* (Farrar, Straus and Giroux, 2007), and 'Mixed Chorus' from *At the Foundling Hospital* (Farrar, Straus and Giroux, 2016), by permission of the author.

**Shazea Quraishi**: 'Fallujah, Basra' from *The Art of Scratching* (Bloodaxe Books, 2015).

**Claudia Rankine**: 'The Health of Us' originally appeared on *LitHub*, by permission of the author. **Roger Robinson**: 'Nightshift' appeared on the dub poetry album *Dog Heart City* on Jahtari Records 2017, published by permission of the author. **Amali Rodrigo**: 'The Eye', 'Peace' and 'Kolmanskop' from *Lotus Gatherers* (Bloodaxe Books, 2016).

**K. Satchidanandan**: 'The Standing Man' and 'The Kiss', translated by the poet from the Malayalam. **Arundhathi Subramaniam**: 'Prayer' and 'Madras, November, 1995' from *Where I Live: New and Selected Poems* (Bloodaxe Books, 2009). **Fadwa Suleiman**: extract from 'Genesis', translated by Marilyn Hacker. **Brian Turner**: 'Horses' originally appeared in *The Massachusetts Review*, and 'The Buddhas of Bamyan' was originally read at the Rotterdam Festival for Poetry International, by permission of the author.

**Mai Der Vang**: 'Transmigration' from *Afterland*, copyright © 2017 by Mai Der Vang, reprinted with the permission of The Permissions Company, Inc. on behalf of Graywolf Press, Minneapolis, Minnesota, www.graywolfpress.org.

**Benjamin Zephaniah**: 'I Have a Scheme' from *Propa Propaganda* (Bloodaxe Books, 1996).

215

# BIOGRAPHIES

**John Agard** was born and educated in Guyana and moved to the UK in 1977. His latest collection is *Playing the Ghost of Maimonides*. Awards include the Casa de las Americas Poetry Prize and the 2012 Queen's Gold Medal for Poetry.

**Elizabeth Alexander** is a renowned poet, essayist, playwright and scholar who is a professor at Columbia University and Director of Creativity and Free Expression at the Ford Foundation. Her *American Blue: Selected Poems* was published by Bloodaxe in 2006. Her latest book is a memoir, *The Light of the World*. She read her 'Praise Song for the Day' at the inauguration of President Barack Obama in 2009.

**Lauren K. Alleyne** is the author of *Difficult Fruit* (Peepal Tree Press, 2014). Alleyne is Assistant Director of the Furious Flower Poetry Center and an Associate Professor of English at James Madison University. Awards include a 2017 Philip Freund Prize in Creative Writing from Cornell University.

**Moniza Alvi** was born in Pakistan and grew up in Hertfordshire. Her most recent poetry book *At the Time of Partition* (Bloodaxe Books, 2013) focused on the partition of India and Pakistan and was shortlisted for the T.S. Eliot Prize. She lives in Norfolk where she tutors for the Poetry School.

**Raymond Antrobus** has published two pamphlets of poems: *Shapes & Disfigurements of Raymond Antrobus* (Burning Eye Books, 2012), and *To Sweeten Bitter* (Out-Spoken Press, 2017). He is a fellow of The Complete Works, and his debut collection will be published by Penned In The Margins in 2018.

**James Berry** (1924-2017) emigrated from Jamaica in 1948 after working in America for a period. One of the first black writers in Britain to achieve wider recognition, Berry rose to prominence in 1981 when he won the National Poetry Competition. His retrospective, *A Story I Am In: Selected Poems* (Bloodaxe Books, 2011), draws on five previous collections, including *Windrush Songs*, published in 2007 to mark the 200th anniversary of the abolition of the slave trade.

**Malika Booker** is a British Caribbean poet, who founded Malika's Poetry Kitchen. *Pepper Seed*, published by Peepal Tree Press in 2013 was longlisted for the OCM Bocas prize and shortlisted for the Seamus Heaney Centre Prize. A selection of her work is published in *Penguin Modern Poets 3* (2017).

**Kevin Bowen** is a poet, painter, and translator. A veteran of the war in Vietnam and former director of the William Joiner Center for the Center of War and Social Consequences at UMass Boston his recent titles include *Thai Binh/ Great Peace*, and, with Nora Paley, *A Grace Paley Reader*.

**Jean 'Binta' Breeze** is a popular Jamaican Dub poet and storyteller. She has released seven poetry books, including *The Fifth Figure* (2006), *Third World Girl: Selected Poems* (2011, with DVD) and *The Verandah Poems* (2016) with Bloodaxe, as well as several records and CDs.

**Jericho Brown** is the recipient of fellowships from the John Simon Guggenheim Foundation and the Radcliffe Institute for Advanced Study at Harvard University. His poems have appeared in *The New York Times* and *The New Yorker*. His most recent book is *The New Testament* (Copper Canyon, 2014).

**Vahni Capildeo** is a Trinidadian British writer interested in cross-genre work and multi-lingualism. Her books include *Measures of Expatriation* (Carcanet, 2016), winner of the Forward Prize for Best Collection, *Simple Complex Shapes*, and *Utter*. She contributes a regular report to *PN Review*.

**Kayo Chingonyi** was born in Zambia in 1987 and moved to the UK at the age of six. He is the author of *Kumukanda* (Chatto, 2017), and is a fellow of The Complete Works. In 2012, he was awarded a Geoffrey Dearmer Prize, and was Associate Poet at the Institute of Contemporary Arts in 2015.

Born in London, England, **Fred D'Aguiar** grew up in Guyana. His most recent books are, the novel, *Children of Paradise* (Granta), and the poetry collection, *The Rose of Toulouse* (Carcanet). He teaches at UCLA.

**Rishi Dastidar** is a fellow of The Complete Works, a consulting editor at *The Rialto* magazine, and a member of the Malika's Poetry Kitchen collective. His debut collection *Ticker-tape* is published by Nine Arches Press.

**Kwame Dawes** is the author of 22 books of poetry and numerous other books of fiction, criticism, and essays. His most recent collection, *City of Bones: A Testament* (Northwestern University Press), appeared in 2017. He teaches at the University of Nebraska and the Pacific MFA Program, is Director of the African Poetry Book Fund and Artistic Director of the Calabash International Literary Festival.

**Toi Derricotte**'s most recent book is *The Undertaker's Daughter*. Her honours include the 2012 Paterson Poetry Prize for Sustained Literary Achievement and the 2012 PEN/Voelcker Award for Poetry. She co-founded Cave Canem with Cornelius Eady in 1996, and serves on the Academy of American Poets' Board of Chancellors.

**Imtiaz Dharker** is a poet, artist and documentary film-maker. Awarded the Queen's Gold Medal for Poetry in 2014, her collections include *Postcards from god*, *I speak for the devil*, *The terrorist at my table*, *Leaving Fingerprints* and *Over the Moon*, all from Bloodaxe in the UK.

**Natalie Diaz** was born in the Fort Mojave Indian Village in Needles, California. She is the author of *When My Brother Was an Aztec* (Copper Canyon, 2012). Awards include the Nimrod/Hardman Pablo Neruda Prize for Poetry, the Louis Untermeyer Scholarship in Poetry from Bread Loaf and a Lannan Fellowship.

**Edward Doegar**'s poems, translations and reviews have appeared in various magazines including *Poetry Review*, *Poetry London* and *Modern Poetry in Translation*. He is a fellow of The Complete Works and his pamphlet, *For Now*, is published by Clinic.

**Rita Dove** has published numerous books, including the Pulitzer Prize-winning *Thomas and Beulah* (1986), the 'novel in verse' *Sonata Mulattica* (2009) and, in 2016, *Collected Poems 1974-2004*. The former US Poet Laureate is Commonwealth Professor of English at the University of Virginia.

**McDonald Dixon** is a Caribbean Writer, born on the island of St Lucia. His work has appeared in *Caribbean Quarterly, Bim, Calabash, Caribbean Writer, Wasafari and Agenda*. In addition to poetry Dixon has written several plays, published three novels and a collection of short stories.

**Ian Duhig** was born in London of Irish Catholic parents, and now lives in Leeds. He won the National Poetry Competition twice, in 1987 and 2001, and the Forward Prize for Best Poem in 2001. Named as one of the Poetry Society's New Generation Poets, his most recent collection is *The Blind Roadmaker* (2016).

**Camille T. Dungy** is the author of four collections of poetry, most recently *Trophic Cascade*, and the essay collection *Guidebook to Relative Strangers*. She is the editor of *Black Nature: Four Centuries of African American Nature Poetry*, and is a professor at Colorado State University.

Poet/Playwright/Songwriter **Cornelius Eady** was born in Rochester, NY, in 1954 and is the author of several collections including *Victims of the Latest Dance Craze*, winner of the 1985 Lamont Prize. He co-founded Cave Canem with Toi Derricotte in 1996. His awards include fellowships from the Guggenheim and Rockefeller Foundations.

Born in Nigeria, **Inua Ellams** is an award winning poet, playwright & founder of the Midnight Run. His books are published by Flipped Eye, Akashic, Nine Arches & Oberon. Identity, Displacement & Destiny are reoccurring themes in his work in which he mixes the traditional with the contemporary.

**Martín Espada**'s latest collection is *Vivas to Those Who Have Failed* (2016). Other books include *The Trouble Ball* (2011), *The Republic of Poetry* (2006), and *Alabanza* (2003). He has received the Shelley Memorial Award, the PEN/Revson Fellowship and a Guggenheim Fellowship.

**Bernardine Evaristo** is the British-Nigerian award-winning author of seven books and numerous works that span the genres of novels, verse fiction, poetry, short fiction, essays, criticism, and radio and theatre drama. She is Professor of Creative Writing at Brunel University London, and founded The Complete Works and the Brunel International African Poetry Prize. She was made an MBE in the Queen's Birthday Honours List 2009.

**Tarfia Faizullah** was born in Brooklyn, NY. She is the author of *Registers of Illuminated Villages* (Graywolf, 2018) and *Seam* (SIU, 2014). Her poems are published widely in periodicals. In 2016, she was recognized by Harvard Law School as one of 50 Women Inspiring Change.

**Nikky Finney** is the author of *On Wings Made of Gauze*, *RICE*, *The World Is Round*, and *Head Off & Split*, which won the National Book Award for Poetry in 2011. She holds the

John H. Bennett, Jr., Chair in Creative Writing and Southern Letters at the University of South Carolina in Columbia.

**Carolyn Forché** is Director of the Lannan Center for Poetry and Poetics and University Professor at Georgetown University in Washington, DC, as well as Visiting Professor at Newcastle University. Her books include the collections *The Country Between Us* (1981), *The Angel of History* (1994) and *Blue Hour* (2003), and two landmark anthologies, *Against Forgetting: Twentieth-Century Poetry of Witness* (1993) and *Poetry of Witness: The Tradition in English: 1500-2001* (2014), edited with Duncan Wu.

**Bashabi Fraser**'s collections include *The Homing Bird* (2017) and *Letters to My Mother and Other Mothers* (2015). She has won several awards and is Professor of English and Creative Writing, Director, Scottish Centre of Tagore Studies (ScoTs), Edinburgh Napier University.

**Ross Gay** was born in Youngstown, Ohio. He is the author of *Catalog of Unabashed Gratitude* (2015), winner of the Kingsley Tufts Award and a finalist for the National Book Award and the National Books Critics Circle Award, and *Bringing the Shovel Down* (2011). He teaches at Indiana University.

Poet, activist, mother, and professor, **Nikki Giovanni** is the acclaimed, award-winning author of 27 books. She is University Distinguished Professor of English at Virginia Tech and reads her work all around the world.

**Aracelis Girmay** is the author of the poetry collections *Teeth*, *Kingdom Animalia*, and *The Black Maria*. Girmay has been awarded fellowships from Cave Canem, the NEA, Civitella Ranieri, and the Whiting Foundation. She teaches and lives in New York.

**Rigoberto González** is the author of 17 books of prose and poetry, most recently *Unpeopled Eden*, awarded the Lenore Marshall Prize from the Academy of American Poets. He is professor of English at Rutgers-Newark, the State University of New Jersey.

**Marilyn Hacker** is the author of 13 books of poems, most recently *A Stranger's Mirror: New and Selected Poems 1995-2014* (W.W. Norton & Company, 2015) as well as a collaborative book *DiaspoRenga* written with Deema K.Shehabi (Holland Park Press, London, 2014), and 16 collections of translations.

**Nathalie Handal** is a French-American poet originally of a Palestinian family from Bethlehem. She is the author of the poetry collections *The Neverfield* (1999), *The Lives of Rain* (2005) and *Love and Strange Horses* (2010), winner of the 2011 Gold Medal Independent Publisher Book Award.

**Choman Hardi** was born in Kurdistan, and sought refuge in the UK in 1993. She is chair of English at the American University of Iraq in Sulaimani. She has published collections of poetry in Kurdish and two in English from Bloodaxe, *Life for Us* (2004), and *Considering the Women* (2015), which was shortlisted for the Forward Prize for Best Collection.

**Joy Harjo** was born in Tulsa, Oklahoma, and is a member of the Muscogee (Creek) Nation. She has written ten books of poetry. Her honours include a Lifetime Achievement Award from the Native Writers Circle of the Americas, and a Wallace Stevens Award from the Academy of American Poets.

**Terrance Hayes** has published five collections, including *How to Be Drawn* (2015), *Lighthead* (2010) and *Hip Logic* (2002). His honours include a Whiting Writers' Award and Guggenheim and MacArthur fellowships. He has taught at Carnegie Mellon University and the University of Pittsburgh, and now lives in New York.

**Kendel Hippolyte** is an award-winning St Lucian poet and playwright. In 2000 he was awarded the St Lucia Medal of Merit for Contribution to the Arts. In 2013 he won the poetry category of the OCM Bocas Prize for Caribbean Literature for his 2012 poetry collection *Fault Lines*.

**Fanny Howe** is the author of more than 20 books of poetry and prose. Her *Selected Poems* (2000) won the 2001 Lenore Marshall Poetry Prize. In 2001 and 2005, Howe was shortlisted for the Griffin Poetry Prize. She was awarded the Ruth Lilly Poetry Prize in 2009.

**Sarah Howe** is a poet, academic and editor. Her first book, *Loop of Jade* (Chatto & Windus, 2015), won the T.S. Eliot Prize and the Sunday Times / PFD Young Writer of the Year Award. She was the founding editor of *Prac Crit*, an online journal of poetry and criticism.

**Ishion Hutchinson** was born in Port Antonio, Jamaica. He has published two collections, *Far District* (2010) and *House of Lords and Commons* (2016). He teaches in the graduate writing program at Cornell University.

**Major Jackson** has published four collections, including *Roll Deep* (2015), hailed in the *New York Times Book Review* as 'a remixed odyssey.' A recipient of a Guggenheim Fellowship, he is the Richard A. Dennis Green & Gold Professor at the University of Vermont. He serves as the Poetry Editor of *The Harvard Review*.

**Honorée Fanonne Jeffers** is the author of four collections, including *The Glory Gets*. She has won poetry fellowships from the Witter Bynner Foundation through the Library of Congress, and the National Endowment for the Arts. She lives in Oklahoma.

Born in Detroit, **Tyehimba Jess** earned his BA from the University of Chicago and his MFA from New York University. He is the author of *leadbelly* (2005) and *Olio* (2016), winner of the Pulitzer Prize. His honours include a Whiting Writers' Award and a Chicago Sun-Times Poetry Award.

**Linton Kwesi Johnson** was born in Jamaica and is a dub poet, author and journalist in London. A selection of his poetry, entitled *Mi Revalueshanary Fren*, was published in 2002 as a Penguin Modern Classics edition, the second living poet and the only black poet to be included in the series. In 2014 he was given an Order of Distinction.

**Ilya Kaminsky** was born in Odessa, Ukraine and lives in the USA. His collection, *Dancing in Odessa*, was translated and published in over a dozen languages. He is co-editor of *The Ecco Anthology of International Poetry* (HarperCollins). *Deaf Republic* (Graywolf Press, 2019) is forthcoming.